MW01153543

COLOR
for
INTERIOR
ARCHITECTURE

COLOR *for* INTERIOR ARCHITECTURE

MARY C. MILLER

JOHN WILEY & SONS, INC.
NEW YORK / CHICHESTER / WEINHEIM / BRISBANE / TORONTO / SINGAPORE

This text is printed on acid-free paper.

Library of Congress Cataloging-in-Publication Data

Miller, Mary C.
Color for interior architecture / Mary C. Miller.
p. cm.
Includes bibliographical references and index.
ISBN 0-471-12736-1 (pbk. : alk. paper)
1. Color . 2. Color in interior decoration. I. Title.
QC495.M47 1997
729—DC21 96-47402

Printed in the United States of America

10 9 8 7 6 5 4 3 2 1

CONTENTS

PREFACE

This book is about the color world of the architectural interior—color that extends in front of and behind you, to either side of you, and above and beneath you. It is about:

- what color is and how you see it;
- the dynamics of color and light in interior space;
- optical and harmonic color interactions;
- interior color quality, illumination, and reflective surfaces;
- interior color as bearer of meaning.

It is intended for students of interior design and architecture, whether in school or out. Its goal is to foster:

- color awareness and a broader vocabulary of colors to see and use;
- technical expertise in the use of color as an instrument;
- a knowledge base of pertinent information on what color is, why it happens, and how to control it;
- increased delight in the aesthetic experience of color.

This book is an outgrowth of my years of teaching color to students in basic design classes and is my response to student questions not only about how-to but about why and so-what. The so-what questions were particularly challenging. What did the small color exercises and experiments we carried out in the studio have to do with the color of an interior wall? How could the idea of advancing and receding color be used to advantage in interior space? These and other questions that arose concerning interior color quality and color use have prompted me to explore and develop the topics addressed in this book.

The ability to understand and control color may be facilitated if one understands what color is, why it happens, and how we see it—in other words, color theory. This book is offered in the hope that it might help to bridge the distance between color theory and color use.

Although all educational programs in interior and architectural design deal with color in some manner, it often receives relatively little attention in comparison with the time and effort devoted to form and function. Color is often taught as a separate course, with little attempt made to relate it to structure.

At whatever program level color theory is introduced, increased color understanding will enable students to make more mature color judgments as they advance through the program.

There is much diversity of opinion on the teaching of color, with little consensus on which learning experiences are appropriate for beginning and advanced levels of a design education program or the sequence in which they should occur. There are different opinions regarding what subject matter to teach and how to make the connection between color in theory and color for interior use.

Should beginning students be introduced to color theory on the assumption that it provides them with a color vocabulary with which to think, or is color theory too abstract to have meaning for them? Are beginning students capable of relating color theory to interior use? Or should theory be deferred until the upper levels of a design program when students are, presumably, more mature?

Should first-year students begin their study of color by building upon where they are and using the colors that they have already learned are appropriate? If so, will the "why" questions emerge as they mature and confront challenges, or will students come to rely mainly on taste, intuition, and market trends?

In my opinion color can be incorporated into every level of the design curriculum and color theory can be discovered by both beginning and mature students if they are given assignments that lead them to discovery.

Given the enormous body of literature on the science and technology of color, what does the designer need to know? Few designers or design students have the background in science and mathematics necessary to read the scientific literature, so pertinent information needs to be translated into less technical language.

Available information on the use of color in design, by and large, assumes a flat surface, such as a painting or print graphics, leaving students of architecture or interior design on their own to make the conceptual leap between these and the unique requirements of color within the three-dimensional enclosure.

This book will assist the design student to make some of these critical connections. It structures color information in such a way that the various aspects can be dealt with logically and sequentially. It provides a basis for color choices based on knowledge while recognizing the importance of intuition and aesthetic judgment.

WHAT THIS BOOK IS ABOUT

Chapter 1 is an introduction to the physical aspects of color in light and on surfaces, the perception of color, the idea of color as energy, and color as symbol.

Chapters 2 and 3 are concerned with legibility and illusion in interior space. Chapter 2 examines the use of advancing and receding color to alter the apparent size and proportions of interior space and objects and to create the illusion of depth on a plane surface. Chapter 3 deals with the role of brightness differences in the perception of form, depth, and location and how depth cues can be manipulated to affect the apparent dimensions of the enclosure. The ability to control both advancing and receding color and the cues by which we read depth can provide the designer with a powerful means for both increasing environment legibility and creating illusion.

Chapter 4 deals with how color, form, depth, and movement information is processed within the visual system and how each stage in the processing of visual information in some way affects what we see. It is a prelude to Chapters 5 and 6, which are concerned with the optical and harmonic interactions of color. A color never appears alone but always within the context of other color, and adjacencies and progressions are critical. These chapters deal with fine-tuning the ability to see color, to make fine color discriminations, and to control color interactions. In Chapter 5 optical color interactions are found to create drastic changes in colors that appear together, and the role of edges is emphasized. Chapter 6 examines harmonic relationships among colors—consonance, dissonance, and discord. Color interactions often make color relationships more important than individual colors themselves.

Chapter 7 discusses the relationship between surface color and light. The chapter is a prelude to Chapters 8 and 9, which deal with color quality, illumination, and the influence of texture on color. Full-spectrum surface color and light as well as control of the values and saturation levels of hues are key to color quality in interiors as well as in the natural world. Color for the interior, therefore, cannot be dealt with apart from illumination. Chapter 8 examines background surface color quality and ways to achieve it. Chapter 9 discusses the effects of natural and electric illumination on color and ways in which surface materials and textures affect color and light.

Chapter 10 is concerned with symbolic meanings attributed to color and the mental image of color we develop with experience. Even though we all have the same type of visual systems, we do not all see interior color in the same way. The initial response to interior color is in terms of its symbolic meanings, which are based on personal experiences and influenced by culture. Our mental image of color determines how we see and use it. Color trends develop when enough people share a common mental image of color; trends change with changes in public mood, trend cycles occurring on a more or less predictable bell curve.

INTRODUCTION

THE EDUCATED EYE

Although we have lived with color and made color choices since infancy, we take for granted the greater part of what we see and make many color decisions unconsciously. The more aware we become of the many nuances of color, the greater our ability to make wonderful color choices.

Color decisions for interiors are exceptionally complex, often fraught with surprise and hazardous pitfalls, even for professional designers with years of experience. It is widely accepted that good taste alone is not an adequate basis for making interior color choices, especially for buildings that house complex functions and a diversity of people.

Although color decisions cannot be based solely on information and reasoning, knowledge and technical expertise are basic to understanding interior color. The student or designer with little or no background in color theory is no better prepared to make interior color decisions than the untutored layperson with good taste, and is vulnerable to fads and unsubstantiated claims, and market pressures.

Knowledge, however, does not negate the necessity for an innate, intuitive color sense, a sensitivity to the psychological and symbolic aspects of color, and confidence in personal aesthetic judgment.

This book is based on the assumption that color awareness and understanding fosters expertise in its use. It is not a book of answers or formulas for "good" color use.

COLOR FOR MIND AND SPIRIT

All surfaces and objects within the interior enclosure have color—vivid and vibrant, neutral, or drab and dingy, but color nevertheless.

Whatever practical uses interior color may serve, its ultimate purpose is to elevate the spirit, to make life more enjoyable. Color is the music of design, and, as with music, mastery of color use requires both intellect and artistry; discipline and experience must augment innate talent. Aesthetics, once the *raison d' etre* for interior design, has been eclipsed by more recent emphasis on the functional and behavioral implications of the designed environment. Aesthetics has been downplayed as outdated Gestalt theory, decorating has been dubbed as cosmetic, and both regarded as superficial.

The impact of the visual environment on our psychological and spiritual well-being, however, must be taken seriously. By engaging us with our surroundings, color contributes to our sense of being alive and aware. Color affects how we feel about ourselves and others, and "good" color is presumed to promote satisfying human relationships and to make the mundane tasks of life more enjoyable.

Insight into what color is, what causes it to happen, and how we perceive it can teach us something about how to create satisfying color for eye, mind, and spirit in the interiors where we spend the greater part of our lives. Interior color is also an important means of communication, proclaiming to others something about our identity and aspirations.

BEGINNING DESIGN COURSES

An instructor is often faced with the formidable task of having to invent a beginning design course from "scratch," with meager support from either texts or tradition. According to Rau and Wright in a study of schools of architecture in western Europe in 1975, the design instructor must respond to the challenge with "experience, sophisticated thought, and dedication if he takes his job seriously." The instructor is faced with the formidable task of either reinventing the world each time the course is taught or else stagnating by continually repeating what was learned as a student. The instructor is on his own.

There is remarkably little communication regarding beginning design courses among the architecture and interior design faculties who teach them, yet project ideas may get "caught" like a cold as they pass from person to person and school to school. It is often impossible to know where projects originate and, therefore, to acknowledge their source.

Rau and Wright noted this lack of communication among design faculties who teach beginning design courses, and how it can discourage the exchange of ideas and even undermine the self-confidence needed for the task (Rau and Wright, 1975, p. 15). In my experience there is little reason to believe that this situation differs greatly from that among schools of architecture and interior design at the present time.

Arcitecture programs, with their emphasis on function and structure, sometimes appear to skirt the question of color completely—all projects are presented in pristine white. Interior design programs frequently rely on furniture, wall treatments, curtains, carpeting, and other artifacts with symbolic content as vehicles for teaching color, thereby minimizing the dynamic role of color and color interactions in the interior. Regard for color solely as a decorative element can obscure its role in environment legibility and illusion.

It is within this context that this book is conceived and written.

• ■ •

1 WHAT IS COLOR?

You live in a colored environment. The sky is sometimes deep azure, sometimes pale blue, sometimes gray or white, and sometimes fiery red, yellow, or pink. Depending on the time of year, foliage is greens, reds, and yellows. Cities often surround you with the grays of concrete and steel and with billboards and advertising in crashing colors to attract your attention. Indoors you could be surrounded by any conceivable color.

So having lived in a colored world throughout your life, would it surprise you to learn that the environment is colorless? Would it also surprise you to find that your eye is not what sees color?

Color vision is a complex process. In order for color to happen, a chain of both "out there" events in the world outside ourselves and "in here" events in our eyes and brains must take place. The "out there" causes of color are illumination and reflective surfaces; the "in here" causes lie within the visual system and the brain's vast network of interacting neurons, which not only repond to visual stimuli, but decode and make sense out of it.

COLOR IS LIGHT

RADIANT AND AMBIENT LIGHT

Color originates in light. *Radiant light* is energy emanated from a light source, such as the sun or a light bulb. The radiant light of the sun travels through the blackness of space at about 186,000 miles per second, arriving here in about eight and a half minutes. It remains invisible until it illuminates a planet or a moon, making it glow in the dark, or until it penetrates the earth's atmosphere, creates daylight, and falls on a surface.

When radiant sunlight reaches the earth's atmosphere, most of it gets bounced around from molecule to molecule and from particle to particle and becomes dispersed. This dispersed light is *ambient light*.

Radiant energy is the cause of illumination. Although light is invisible, when it illuminates particles in the atmosphere, some wavelengths are absorbed while others are reflected. The sky is blue because moisture in the atmosphere scatters the short or blue wavelengths, but the longer red wavelengths pass through it (Kuehni, 1983, p. 19). You can see rainbows or shafts of light only because light is reflected and refracted by particles of moisture or dust in the air.

Because of the atmosphere and ambient light, life on earth is possible. Ambient light illuminates the day and makes objects and surfaces visible. Without ambient light the world would be like the airless moon. The sky would be black and surfaces receiving direct light would be burned to a crisp, while those in shade and shadow would be pitch black and frozen.

Some radiant light comes through the atmosphere, and is seen as areas of direct sunlight. Ambient light illuminates shade and shadow areas that receive light only indirectly. Although ambient light is no more visible than the radiant sunlight that is constantly present in the black night sky, it carries information about forms and surfaces because they reflect light differentially.

SPECTRAL LIGHT

Color originates in light, but if the light does not contain wavelengths that can be reflected by surfaces, there is no color. If you do not believe this, observe what happens to green grass and red and blue flowers under a sodium vapor street light. Because there are no green, red, or blue wavelengths in this light, these colors appear to be only a dirty gray.

The white light from the sun is actually a complex bundle of visible and invisible *wavelengths*. When sunlight is directed through a prism, the different wavelengths are separated from one another, and appear as a band of brilliantly colored *spectral hues* (Color Art 1). The hues that appear most clearly to the eye are violet, indigo (violet blue), cyan (blue green), green, yellow, orange, and red (De Grandis, 1986, p. 13).

Spectral hues may also be seen in a rainbow. Each droplet of moisture suspended in the atmosphere serves as a tiny prism, and these aggregate to convert the sky into a colossal prism. From where you are standing, each droplet of moisture refracts the light at a certain angle, and together they separate white light into its component hues.

Wavelengths are measured in nanometers, a nanometer being one billionth of a meter. The visible spectrum falls within the range of approximately 380 to 770 nanometers. Violet comes into visibility at around 400 nanometers, next to the ultraviolet part of the spectrum. As the wavelengths increase, cyan, green, yellow, orange and red hues appear. Red disappears from visibility at around 700 nanometers as it gives way to infrared wavelengths (IESNA Color Committee, 1990, p. 2) (Color Art 1*A*).

Although these hues are clearly discernible, the transitions from one to another are gradual—more like a glissando on a violin string than the distinct notes of a piano scale. Authorities, therefore, differ somewhat as to exact color names. The terms red, orange-red, or orange may be used to identify the long wavelengths of the spectrum, and violet, violet-blue, blue-violet, indigo, or blue to identify the short wavelengths. With somewhat less ambiguity, green and yellow identify the medium wavelengths. In this book we shall use the terms *violet-blue, cyan, green, yellow, and orange-red* to identify the hues in the sunlight spectrum, although, for the sake of simplicity, there are times when we may use the term "red" as short for orange-red and blue as short for violet-blue or cyan.

The visible wavelengths of the sunlight spectrum comprise only a small segment of a much larger band of wavelengths. We are blind to wavelengths outside the visible spectrum, such as ultraviolet, infrared, and radio wavelengths, gamma rays, and X-rays.

Bees see flowers in reflected ultraviolet light, and some animals see things in ultraviolet or infrared light. Other animals are insensitive to some of the spectral rays that we see, which is why "bug lights" do not attract mosquitoes. What wonders we might behold if our eyes were sensitive to the infrared or ultraviolet wavelengths that surfaces reflect! The night could be ablaze with color emanating from planets and stars. Flowers, minerals in the soil, your own teeth and nails, numerous manufactured products, and some paints could glow with amazing colors.

But what happens when spectral light falls upon a color surface?

LIGHT FROM REFLECTED SURFACES

Color in the environment is characterized by *brightness* and *hue,* Color is a general term that includes both brightness and hue, although it is popularly thought of as meaning hue.

- Brightness is determined by the *amount* of light emitted by a light source and reflected by a surface.
- Hue is determined by the *kind* of light—the particular wavelengths in light—emitted by a light source and selectively reflected by a surface.

Hue

In daylight, if you have normal vision, you see the world as color surfaces. As you will find in Chapter 7, color surfaces selectively reflect certain of the visible wavelengths in light and absorb all the others. Reflected wavelengths determine the hues that we see.

Color in the environment depends on:

- *wavelengths* in light emitted by a light source and
- *surfaces* that selectively absorb and reflect them.

Hue transforms what would otherwise be a black, white, and gray scene into a world of color and life. The addition of hue to forms and surfaces in the environment has been likened to the addition of water color to a drawing, perhaps an evolutionary afterthought, since many animals, including your pets, are hue blind.

The basic hues in pigment or surface color are the same basic hues as those in light. There are infinite ways in which basic hues can be intermixed to create an infinite range and variety of colors.

Brightness

Even though sunlight contains all of the wavelengths required for hue vision, it is colorless. The amount of this colorless light falling on a color surface and reflected from it determines whether it will appear darker or lighter.

Brightness refers to the amount of light illuminating a surface:

- The more light a surface receives, the brighter it will appear.
- The less light a surface receives, the darker it will appear.

Value is the darkness or lightness of the surface:

- The lighter or whiter the surface color, the more light it reflects and the brighter it will appear.
- The darker or blacker the surface, the more light it absorbs and the darker it will appear.

Snow is black in the darkness of night, and coal can appear white in dazzling sunlight. Without light there is only blackness; according to the old adage, all cats are black in the dark.

As you will find in Chapter 3, surface brightness differences are our most important visual cue. Brightness differences enable us to see the forms of objects, to distinguish things from their backgrounds, and to navigate our way through the environment.

Brightness differences enable us to discern the darkness or lightness of colors; to see light, shade, and shadow patterns; to read the printed page; or to interpret a black-and-white photograph or movie. With this information the person with impaired hue vision can read the environment quite well.

But what a drab and dismal place the world would be if it were seen only in shades of gray!

COLOR IS A PERCEPTION

Like the tree that falls silently in the forest if there is no ear to hear it, *color does not exist until it is seen.*

"Seeing," however, does not take place in the eye—the eye "sees" neither color nor what is colored. The retina, the light-sensitive area of the eye, is not like a small television screen that registers images.

Incoming light wavelengths only trigger cells in the retina to generate minute electrochemical impulses, which are transmitted to higher levels in the visual system for decoding, organizing, and translating into visual images, the meanings of which are evaluated. Seeing, therefore, occurs *somewhere in the brain.*

In Chapter 4 you will find that the visual system processes brightness information separately from hue information. Brightness and hue, therefore, have their own particular dynamic qualities. We rely primarily on brightness differences to see the world around us, but hue adds color to the picture. Hues interact with one another as hue information is processed through the visual system, the interactions between hues often strongly affecting the appearance of each.

COLOR IS ENERGY

The sun is the ultimate source of all energy and life on earth, but because sunlight is invisible, you may take its power for granted. You sense the heat of a hot summer sun beating down relentlessly on the parched desert at midday, but just imagine all of the brilliant spectral hue inherent in that white light!

The energy in sunlight is easier to comprehend when you isolate and make visible the brilliant individual color components that constantly envelop you. If white sunlight is invisible energy, the colors reflected from surface color or filtered through a colored gel are visible energy. If light is directed through color filters, such as a sheet of colored gel, only those wavelengths that correspond to the color of the filter can pass through it—all other wavelengths are blocked. The more saturated the color of the filter, the more brilliant is the spot of color in the filtered light. The colored gel does not stain the light—the wavelengths of the color that you see in all if its brilliance *already exist in the light*.

The energy in sunlight is also visible when brilliant surface hues are illuminated. However vivid a surface color appears to the eye, its brilliance is possible only because the wavelengths in the light that illuminates it are correspondingly brilliant.

Whenever you use a verb to indicate what color *does,* you are affirming the energy inherent in light and color:

- Colors *advance* or *recede.*
- Color *affects* the sizes, shapes, and location of things and the sizes and shapes of enclosures.
- Colors *interact* with each other.
- Color *affects* the mood of the viewer; it *delights* or *depresses,* it *stimulates* or *calms,* and so on.
- White wall surfaces *expand* the space, whereas black walls *close in on you* like the night.

Whatever colors *do* are manifestations of the energy and power that light and color *bring* to an interior. Each color reflected from a surface has its own particular energy characteristics, and elicits a particular energy response in the viewer.

All of the color energy inherent in white sunlight enters the daylit interior. How much color, how much visible energy do you want reflected from walls and other surfaces? How much and what kind of stimulation is desired in the interiors where you live and work?

The effects of the energy of color and light on the spatial quality of an interior are discussed in Chapter 2. Color and light can alter the appearance of interior space, enhance legibility, and create illusion within the interior enclosure. Chapter 3 considers the role of brightness vision in our perception of depth and the spatial quality of the interior, the forms, and the location of things.

Chapters 5 and 6 are concerned with how colors interact with one another—Chapter 5 with optical interactions, and Chapter 6 with harmonic interactions. Color interactions can be drastic and dynamic. They can change not only the appearance of the colors themselves, but the appearance of what is colored.

Color energy within an interior enclosure, however, is determined predominantly by color on large surfaces. Chapter 7 examines the physical bases of color composition, while more down-to-earth aspects of interior color selection and paint mixing are considered in Chapter 8.

Chapter 9 is concerned with how interior color derives from illumination, and how both color and illumination interact with reflective materials.

COLOR IS COMMUNICATION

COLOR AS SYMBOL

Color is communication—a language all its own. With color you can communicate an enormous variety of messages.

Your immediate response to color is in terms of what it means, what it "says" to you. As you will find in Chapter 10, color has meaning because you *attribute* meaning to it. Because seeing is a matter of translating what you see into symbolic meanings, color meanings are far easier to grasp than color as an abstract element, which requires intellectual effort. You see and think symbols, therefore, your perception of what color says, what it stands for, how you feel about it is instantaneous.

You do not approach the study of interior color as a novice, but as one who has been living with colored interiors all of your life, and who has developed opinions regarding what is appropriate for certain situations or people or uses. This background provides you with your basis for making color judgments. Broadening your experience in seeing and your knowledge of color should enrich your ability to make interior color choices.

It goes without saying that the broader your experience in observing color and your knowledge of color theory, the richer your visual vocabulary of background color experiences against which to make color judgments.

SYMBOL VERSUS ABSTRACT ELEMENT

Thinking of the interior in terms of *design elements* differs from thinking of it as building and furniture styles, fabric and wallpaper swatches, and curtains and lighting fixtures. It is not that this realistic approach to design is wrong, but tangible objects are so laden with symbolic meanings that it can be difficult to see them any other way, and they can become ends in themselves. Concern for what you want others to think of you, for prestige symbols, for sentimental associations, for appropriateness, or for expressions of identity or aspirations can actually interfere with design as a way to maximize the potential of interior space.

The symbolic meanings of tangible objects are far stronger and easier to grasp than are the dynamic qualities of color, light, form, or space. Regarding design in terms of design elements or color dynamics or interactions may be uncomfortable for some people, particularly those who are very practical or business oriented, or who have not learned to see the environment in this particular way.

Those who regard design as a matter of tangible objects, such as furniture, fabrics, and the like, often do a superb job of putting interiors together. In so doing, however, they are able to look beyond things as things, and are successful in evaluating their sizes, colors, the amount of light in the enclosure, and in dealing with the problem of maximizing the potential of the space—in other words, of thinking in terms of design elements. They may do this unconsciously, relying on their intuitive sense of what works.

Although designing with tangible objects can stimulate innovation, thinking in terms of design elements gives you more freedom to get to the essence of a design problem and to be innovative.

You might think of design elements as the design alphabet with which symbolic statements are constructed, the end product of design always being the visual experience. The interior is always seen in terms of the meanings it conveys, but the concern of this book is how you get to that point.

COLOR IS MAGIC

An interior is not only a place for activities—for *doing*—it is also a place for *being*, and color in an interior can make being there a satisfying and enriching experience. Color can be music to the eyes; it is more relevant to poetry, music, and art than to physics or psychology or behavioral engineering. Transcending function and practicality, color engages feeling before reason and intellect.

The magic of color can transform the ordinary into the exceptional, and that is the magic that we seek.

2 THE DYNAMICS OF INTERIOR COLOR

An interior is a three-dimensional world that completely envelops you in color; color surfaces are all around you, above you, and beneath you. Interior color is, therefore, experienced quite differently from any other color use.

Interior surface color is dynamic energy; it does not sit idly by. Advancing and receding color defines the structure and the space of the enclosure. Color can be used to increase or decrease the legibility of an interior, and is a prime instrument for creating illusion.

Color influences the visual weight, size, and distance of objects and surfaces. Hue and brightness differences separate objects and pattern motifs from their backgrounds and locate them in space, making it possible to see what things are and where they are located.

Pattern not only intrigues the eye and enriches architectural surfaces, it can be more powerful than flat color in affecting the spatial quality of the enclosure.

LEGIBILITY AND ILLUSION

There are two kinds of reality:

- *physical* reality and
- *perceptual* reality.

Physical reality can be measured in feet and inches and weighed in pounds and ounces. Perceptual reality, however, is subjective; it is a matter of how big or how heavy or how far away something appears to be. And one reality is just as "real" as the other.

In the brain's judgment *how it appears is how it is.* If appearance contradicts physical reality, that is known as illusion. We say that the environment is *legible* when physical reality and perceptual reality are the same, when things look like what they "are" and the signals are clear.

LEGIBILITY

A legible interior is easy to read. Things are *what* they seem to be and *where* they seem to be located.

The plan, structure, and details are clear, and you have little difficulty identifying architectural features and furniture, knowing where to go, and navigating your way around obstacles. Stairs are not confused with flat surfaces, and entrances, exits, and functional areas are obvious even to the uninitiated. You can easily identify the forms of things and distinguish them from their backgrounds. A flat surface appears flat, a corner looks like a corner, and a rounded surface appears rounded. If a surface seems uneven, it is because it is uneven.

Legibility makes for a reasonable, undistorted world—a predictable, honest, uncontrived statement of physical reality. There are no lies. Legibility is needed for a stable, reasonable environment, but is of particular importance for those whose eyesight is failing, and wherever safety and efficiency are matters of concern.

Interior designers, architects, and occupants of interior spaces are usually more concerned with legible, easy-to-read environments than with theatrical effects; in fact, contradicting physical reality is seldom an issue in most interiors. However, maximizing the æsthetic and psychological satisfaction that an interior can provide is a primary concern, and this leads us to the subject of illusion.

ILLUSION

Illusion is as important as legibility and is a fact of life whether the environment is legible or not. Legibility and illusion are not mutually exclusive, and must be dealt with simultaneously.

Although the very mention of illusion conjures up notions of theatre, trompe l'oeil, fantasy, Disneyland—all of which deal with deception—we actually deal with illusion every time a wall is painted, a curtain is hung, or an article of furniture is placed in a room. When we alter the appearance of things by the use of color or by manipulating their sizes, shapes, or placement, we are choosing one illusion over another.

Illusion can alter the spatial quality of an enclosure and the apparent forms, sizes, and locations of things. It can shorten the apparent length of an airport corridor, imparting to it a more human dimension and making a long-distance trek seem less tiresome. It can make a huge restaurant or auditorium seem intimate and cozy, or lend an air of spaciousness to a tiny office. Illusion can insinuate space that isn't there by creating the impression of vistas on a flat surface. Illusion is frequently employed to correct an architectural flaw as well as to visually reinforce structural form.

Aside from the illegibility of poor design, illusion at its worst can create safety hazards and disorient the unwary. It can cause people to stumble or bump into things or fear falling. It can make long corridors seem endless. It can camouflage entrances and exits or elevators or stairs, or make a floor surface look like an obstacle course. Extreme examples of illusion are the Halloween "fun house," the "hall of mirrors," and other devices calculated to titillate or terrorize.

Often illusion merely piques the imagination or relieves monotony, and sometimes we bring fantasy and wit to our world by contradicting or exaggerating reality. A practical world devoid of humor and poetics would be a dreadfully boring place.

The magic of a beautiful interior is the successful use of illusion, and perhaps magic is an interior's most important quality. As with any good magic show, however, the techniques for creating illusion should not be evident to the observer.

COLOR DYNAMICS

COLORS THAT ADVANCE AND RECEDE

Colors on interior surfaces can enhance the legibility of the environment or create illusion, because they are perceived to advance and recede. Colors are generally regarded as more advancing as they become:

- lower in value,
- more highly saturated, and
- warmer in hue.

Colors are generally regarded as more receding as they become:

- higher in value,
- lower in saturation, and
- cooler in hue.

Advancing or receding are relative characteristics determined by making comparisons.

- If two advancing colors appear together, one may seem somewhat more advancing than the other.
- If two receding colors appear together, one may seem somewhat more receding than the other.

A color may have both advancing and receding characteristics, depending on which characteristics are dominant in its intermix and which are subordinate. Value, the darkness or lightness of a color, and saturation, its vividness or grayness, can be more important characteristics of a color than hue in determining the spatial quality of color.

- If orange-red, the hottest and most advancing hue, were high in value and low in saturation, it could be described as "pale, grayed pink" with one advancing and two receding characteristics.
- Violet-blue, the coolest and most receding hue, can seem oppressively hot at high-saturation and middle-value ranges; a pale but high saturation blue can appear quite advancing, even more advancing than a low-saturation orange brown.
- Although a highly saturated yellow is the most advancing of all hues, olive drab—a low value, low saturation yellow—is so receding that the army uses it for camouflage.
- Hazy atmospheric conditions make distant mountains appear lighter, grayer, and bluer; therefore, lightness, grayness, and blueness seem to lend distance to any color, making it appear to recede.

A THREE-DIMENSIONAL COLOR FIELD EXPERIMENT

"Hue is a sensory initiator of the experience of space" (Swirnoff, 1988, p. 35). Swirnoff has compared the volumetric quality of colors in a three-dimensional field. Color-aid silk-screened paper was placed in a viewing device, the essence of which was a 6-inch white square board in which a 3-inch square window was cut. Test colors were placed 9 inches behind the window and viewed from a distance of 3 to 6 feet. The frame provided a color context within which the test colors were viewed. Lighting was provided by a Luxo lamp placed so that no shadows were cast on test colors.

Colors viewed through the window were transformed to the quality of film or volume color, which tends to float in space rather than being perceived as belonging to a surface (Swirnoff, 1988, p. 35):

> *...A bright orange-red was chosen initially. The red paper placed against the back plane, 9 inches from the window, was observed as a film through the 3-inch aperture, which it appeared to fill. Within seconds the warm, brilliant red appeared to move from its spatial position within the frame, to float in front of the window opening. In this case the window assumed the appearance of a square field, with the red superimposed or suspended in front of it. The change from surface to film color was perceived, and from a distance greater than 10 feet the spatial illusion was described as a projected light. After prolonged observation, between 30 and 60 seconds, the illusion was intensified, and the red seemed to be located inches in front of the window. In no case did it appear in its true location, at the back plane of the space-frame. (Swirnoff, 1988, p. 37)*

When other colors were tested:

- "...saturated blue appeared more distant from the eye than the saturated red."
- "...the darker cool red and brighter blue were more equivalent in distance, the first in front of and the second behind the window."

- "...a series of desaturated (grayer) blues tended to recede."
- "Dark, fully saturated blue appeared as volume color to some observers."
- "The brightness of a lighter blue "increased, and its location, relative to the darker, saturated blue...appeared to be closer to the eye, but behind the frame."
- "...the spatial behavior of reds and blues is a function of how intense or bright they appear to be... ."
- Mixed and desaturated hues of dark value, such as brown, also had a volumetric appearance.
- "Deep violet was unstable as a volume color. If it contained red, it tended to advance slightly; influenced by blue, on the other hand, it receded in comparison with its blue or brown equivalents."
- "A fully saturated yellow...tends to expand radially, rather than advancing, when observed adjacent to a surrounding white, bright window frame. When observed through a window covered by a dark gray, its brightness increases and the yellow appeared to advance."
- "...brightness or value as well as hue conditions the effect of colors in the center field".

(Permission is granted by Birkhäuser, Boston, to use the text from the chapter "Color, Space and Time" from the book, *Dimensional Color* by Lois Swirnoff, © 1989.)

DYNAMICS OF INTERIOR SURFACE COLOR

Color on interior surfaces provides a powerful means for enhancing the legibility of the interior or for creating illusion. The physical structure holds the building together, but color defines the visual structure (Color Art 2, 3*A–D*, and 4):

> *Color can extend walls, raise ceilings, eliminate corners. Reaching beyond the limits of construction, it can sculpt a new space whose borders are defined purely by the spectrum, whose geometry consists not of carpenters' planes, but of the lines where one hue begins and another one ends... . color creates an architecture all its own. (Kaufman and Dahl, 1992, p.15).*

INTERIOR REGARDED AS ROOM

How you use color in an interior is determined by whether your concept of an interior is that of:

- room or
- space-bounding surfaces and spatial volumes.

A room can totally envelop you in wonderful color, but what does the color do to the space? Color on floors and ceilings affects perceived room height and wall color defines room boundaries.

Boxlike rooms are found in homes, offices, hospitals, schools, and just about everywhere else. Sometimes the intimacy of a small enclosure is desirable, but more often the design challenge is to "get the room out of the box."

Usually the larger the room or the greater the amount of window area, the less the sense of confinement. "Continuous color on all surfaces of a room can exacerbate the sense of confinement, particularly if the room is small, square or nearly so, and if it has no outside view" (Mock, 1946). Advancing color on all surfaces of a room closes in on the viewer to a greater degree than does receding color, which could make the enclosure seem comparatively larger. Advancing colors can impart intimacy to large spaces, such as hotel lobbies or auditoriums, as well as to small, cozy rooms, such as dens or bistros. They may be dramatic in small spaces used for short periods of time, such as foyers or powder rooms. And if it is desirable to emphasize the sense of enclosure, advancing colors may be used successfully in small living rooms (Color Art 5 and 6).

Neutrals and soft receding tints in medium to high values are popular backgrounds, especially for small rooms or where color is not intended to be the star performer. They lie flat on a surface and are nonintrusive, allowing the attention to be directed toward people and their interactions and activities, furnishings, art, the architecture, function, or whatever the occupants consider important (Color Art 7 and 8).

2.1 LIGHT BOX 1

Construct a 4-inch cube with a 1-inch hole in two adjacent faces, one for admitting light and one for looking into the box. Use color, graphics, materials, mirror, or whatever you wish on the inside surfaces to alter the perceived proportions, size, and shape of the enclosure.

If this were a foyer or small room, how would the scale of the surface design be perceived in relation to the enclosure?

2.2 LIGHT BOX 2: A PANORAMA ON THE INTERIOR OF A CUBE (Jo Hasell and Jerald Leimenstoll) (Color Art 2)

Construct a 6-inch cube in which the design is continuous over all six faces of the cube interior. (The cube is formed when the faces of the flattened box are in place.) Your goal is to create an interior environment that is totally independent of the box structure. Pictorial materials from printed sources may be used, or you may paint your own design on the interior surfaces.

INTERIOR REGARDED AS PLANE SURFACES

If you regard interior architecture as separate space-bounding planes, whether it be a room or an open plan, you are at liberty to deal with each surface separately.

How advancing or receding color or pattern is perceived on any architectural plane is determined by the way it relates to the overall context.

Vertical Planes

A change in color with a change in plane can separate adjacent wall surfaces of a room by detaching them at the corners, thereby alleviating the sense of confinement in boxlike rooms. "If a dark or boldly patterned wall stands between two light ones, it will seem quite free in space, but if all four walls are dark, or if all are patterned, the room will seem small" (Mock, 1946).

In an open plan color may be used on individual planes as desired. The harmonic interaction among colors on separate walls is the source of color complexity, and may be preferred by those who prefer smaller amounts of bold colors rather than pattern or tints throughout. As shown in Color Art 9, strong colors are distributed throughout the otherwise white interior. Interactions among solid color areas rather than pattern were chosen for visual variety and interest.

One wall of advancing color surrounded by receding color can be a dominant feature all by itself. Advancing color is effective on walls that stop or deflect movement, such as where a passageway ends or turns a corner. It can draw attention to selected areas, such as reception areas, elevators, or entrances; it can also divert attention away from other areas that should be deemphasized (Color Art 9 and 10).

Wall color can affect the perceived proportions of an enclosure. How would the following affect a square room?

- Advancing or receding color on four walls.
- Advancing color on one wall and receding color on three walls.
- Advancing color on two opposite walls, with receding color on the two between them.
- Advancing color on three walls and receding color on the fourth.

Horizontal Planes

In response to the force of gravity, color and pattern on ceilings and floors is experienced largely in terms of visual weight (Color Art 4, 11, and 8).

Advancing colors on ceilings are perceived to lower ceiling height. The effect is maximized if:

- the same color is used on both floor and ceiling, because the eye tends to associate like colors, and
- receding colors are used on vertical surfaces.

Receding colors are perceived to raise ceiling height. The effect is maximized if:

- receding color is also used on the floor and
- advancing color is used on vertical walls.

White, off-white, or tints on ceilings are the colors lightest in both visual weight and value. They are like sky, the most expansive element in the environment.

High-saturation, dark, and warm colors are often used to lower ceilings. Whereas a "too heavy" ceiling is sensed as threatening, low value hues can be quite dramatic. Despite its high value, a saturated yellow on a ceiling can seem astoundingly heavy.

Floors are the supporting base for everything—the structure, furniture, people, activities. Dark colors identify floors with the earth, the darkest element in the environment. White or near-white floors lend airiness to the enclosure, and can make the furniture seem to "float" (Color Art 10). Mahnke and Mahnke, however, warn that white floors may be "touch inhibiting"—not to be walked on (Mahnke and Mahnke, 1993, p. 16).

The floor may be the largest surface in your field of vision, especially in a large enclosure. Look around the room where you are, and compare the relative amounts of floor and wall surfaces you see.

2.3 INTERIOR MODEL 1
(Michael Kalil) (See the following figures)

Use advancing and receding colors on the various surfaces of identical models to alter the perceived size and proportions of the enclosure in the following ways. Members of a class can develop different options so that comparisons can be made.

a. Increase the apparent depth of the model.
b. Bring the back wall forward.
c. Decrease the apparent width and raise the apparent ceiling height.
d. Increase the apparent width and lower the ceiling.
e. Eliminate the corners.
f. Warp the structure.

Color to Affect the Size, Shape, and Proportions of the Enclosure

a. *All white interior for comparison.*

b. *Enclosure appears narrower and higher.*

c. *Enclosure appears shallower as the back wall is brought forward.*

d. *Enclosure appears wider and shallower and the ceiling appears lower.*

e. *Enclosure appears narrower and deeper and the ceiling appears higher.*

f. *The structure appears warped.*

BUFFER SPACE FOR COLOR

Color and pattern not only affect the size and proportions of a room, they occupy space. A colored or patterned surface may even require its own buffer space. Lively surface color and/or pattern can so fill a room or a building that it does not appear empty even when unfurnished.

The more obtrusive a color or pattern is, the more energy it brings to the interior, and the more space it occupies. Hot, vivid, unusual, or exotic colors, dissonant combinations, or important patterns require more buffer space than do quiet receding colors, and are usually but not always used in small amounts within an enclosure. Vivid chrome yellow, chartreuse, or magenta could be exciting in limited amounts but overpowering in cramped rooms. Such colors are perhaps most successful on a single wall of an interior or on an object, and often within a larger context of white or other neutral background. This is a matter of personal preference but, to repeat a cliché, a little goes a long way.

A patterned surface can be stronger than a solid surface of the same color, and pattern in strong color can be striking, indeed. Despite the fact that "too much" color or pattern for the size of an enclosure may be experienced as overwhelming, by no means does this rule out such use. Consider the living room setting shown in Color Art 5. A living room that completely envelops you in vivid red is accentuated with even more vivid luminous red silk fabrics and red flowers. The room has a sensuously luxurious elegance, is highly stimulating, uniquely individual and uninhibited, but every detail carefully controlled.

2.4 COLOR FOR AN INTERIOR MODEL

Use colors and/or patterns on vertical and horizontal planes in a complex interior model of your own choosing, such as an open plan for an office complex or a public space. Include some ceilings if possible. Consider:

a. functional requirements,
b. areas to be emphasized or deemphasized,
c. colors seen against each other as you move through the space, and
d. the sense of openness or enclosure.

How would the space be experienced from inside? How well do the colors interact with the space?

DYNAMICS OF OBJECT COLOR

THE PERCEPTION OF CROWDEDNESS OR EMPTINESS

Whether you consider a room crowded or spacious depends on the relationship between the volume of space enclosed and the space occupied by people, objects, activities, noise, color, pattern, and so on. "Too small" rooms are probably encountered more frequently than are "too large" rooms, but relating "too large" spaces to human scale is a design concern.

Goodness of fit between the size of a room and its contents is a highly subjective, culturally conditioned matter of personal preference. Some people derive satisfaction from a busy, crowded setting, but too much color or pattern, too many people, too many things, too much going on in a confined space can add up to sensory overload, no matter what your preferences may be. Some cherish pristine, uncluttered space that others would consider empty, cold, barren, and unfriendly. Most people have preferences somewhere in between.

Furnishings, color, and pattern make architecture habitable and personal, and it is important that you become aware of what is for you or for your client a comfortable fit between an enclosure and its contents.

THE PERCEIVED SIZES OF THINGS

If you judge a room to be overcrowded with things, it is because, irrespective of functional requirements, you are sensing the need for a "comfortable" amount of space to contain them. Objects, like colors and people, seem to have their own perceptual space requirements. Generally speaking, the larger, heavier, or more important an object is, the more buffer space it requires.

If furniture seems "too large" or "too small" for the room, or if there is "too much" or "not enough" of it, you have a goodness-of-fit problem. Can color be employed to make the room and its contents more visually compatible with one another? And, if so, to what extent?

Generally speaking:

- Advancing colors make objects appear larger and interior enclosures appear smaller.
- Receding colors make objects appear smaller and interior enclosures appear larger.

Objects and the enclosure derive their scale from one another. Generally speaking:

- A large enclosure makes the furniture appear smaller; a small enclosure makes the furniture appear larger.
- Large furniture makes the enclosure appear smaller; small furniture makes the enclosure appear larger. (See illustration, p.44)

With this in mind, what colors could promote goodness-of-fit between a large grand piano and a "too small" room? What colors should the piano and the background surface be?

VISUAL WEIGHT AND THE IMPORTANCE OF OBJECTS

Visual Weight

In order to have come this far along in life, you have developed a sense of the relationship between the sizes and colors of things and their weights. You, therefore, automatically attribute weight to color, and a colored wall is perceived to have weight in the same way a colored object is perceived to have weight.

- Vivid or dark advancing colors make an object or a wall appear heavier,
- Tints or low saturation color make them appear lighter in weight

Accordingly, a white grand piano should appear to weigh less than a black one, and a grayed blue grand piano less than a red one.

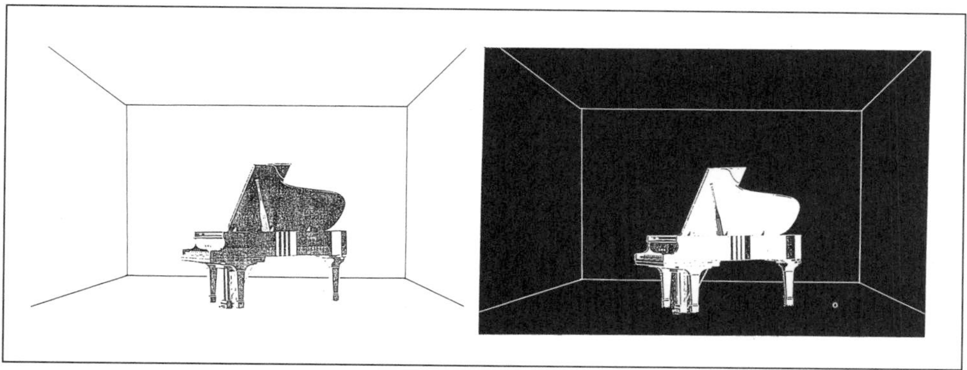

Grand pianos.

Importance

Things may be important because of meanings attributed to them. A sculpture may be such an impressive work of art that it deserves or even demands to be center field in a spacious setting. The statement it makes gives it importance and visual weight disproportionate to its physical size and weight.

Sometimes isolation lends importance to things, even things of lesser value. Sometimes things are important because they are functional, or because they are expensive, or because they are old, or because they are new, or because of associations such as that George Washington slept there.

Sometimes just being huge or tiny or complicated can make things important, but color, ornamentation, or visual size can also lend significance to them.

Greater visibility makes things important, whereas camouflage hides them.

- The more an object's color contrasts with the color of its background, the more visible it becomes;
- The more an object blends into the color of its background, the less visible it becomes (Color Art 13).
- Visual interest elsewhere can divert attention away from an object.

A decision is made, consciously or unconsciously, regarding what you want to be a featured attraction and what you want to camouflage—an antique sofa, a trash can, a water cooler, a painting, a window curtain, the paper towels. Do you want the woodwork or other architectural detail to stand out against the wall color or be a part of it? And what to do about an ungainly sofa—could it be camouflaged if its color or pattern were the same as its background?

A scale model of Gerrit Rietveld's famous Red and Blue Chair of 1918 is shown in Color Art 13. It was painted in the style of a Mondrian painting, so that it is perceived not as the original chair and is no longer at home in its original setting. An environment to reinforce the altered concept of the chair is created. The chair now blends into its new environment and becomes indistinct from it.

BALANCING COLOR SURFACES AND OBJECTS

Visual balance within an interior is a matter of the distribution of the perceptual sizes and weights of color surfaces and objects. Visual balance is not ordinarily a problem until you are confronted with "too big" or "too little" or "too much" or "not enough", which by bothering you lets you know that something is out of kilter.

If you think of balance as a right–left phenomenon, remember that in an interior the difference between right–left and back–front is only a matter of momentary orientation. Because color has visual weight, a dark wall at one end of a room can provide horizontal balance for the grand piano at the opposite end, regardless of which way you are facing.

Vertical imbalance may be experienced as top-heavy or bottom-heavy. Rooms are inevitably bottom-heavy as gravity draws everything to the floor and as dark floor colors emphasize weight. Visual interest in the upper half of the volume of space in a room serves to counter the bottom-heaviness of the enclosure. Paintings, tall plants, decorative ceilings, and other such items above eye level figure importantly in establishing vertical balance, as can a well-chosen ceiling color.

Too heavy color on ceilings can be oppressive and heavy objects suspended over one's head can threaten, regardless of how well attached they may be. Theoretically, top-heavy ought to balance bottom-heavy but is more likely to make you feel mashed. This is particularly noticeable in very wide, expansive enclosures with low ceilings.

A chandelier suspended in space or a mobile that seems to defy gravity and appear to float contributes significantly to vertical balance. The charm of the mobile shown in Color Art 14 lies not only in its wit, elegance, and movement, but also as an object located within the volume of space within the enclosure. If you

2.5 THE OBJECT–ENCLOSURE RELATIONSHIP

In an interior model of your own choosing, place the furnishings in a functional arrangement. Cubes may represent furniture. Experiment with the use of colored or patterned objects and surfaces in the enclosure to create a livable environment, bearing in mind horizontal as well as vertical balance:

a. Fill the space with functional objects, color, and/or pattern to make a livable interior for the person who prefers a crowded, "busy" environment.
b. Taking a minimalist approach, include as few objects and little color or pattern as you think would make an elegant spatial arrangement.

What for you is a "comfortable" relationship between the volume of enclosed space and the objects, color, and pattern required to make it habitable? How large or how small an enclosure makes you feel comfortable? At what point do objects becomer clutter? How much color or pattern is too much? What elements require buffer space? What is the difference between emptiness and spaciousness?

can attribute to objects and colors the sort of mutual gravitational pull that the moon and earth have for one another, or the valence with which one atom attracts another, you can attribute a subtle perceptual attraction between objects and colors within an enclosure. This being the case, an object in the upper half of the space might appear to exert a subtle magnetic pull on an object beneath it, thereby lightening its visual weight. Perhaps that could have been sufficient reason for the chandelier over Liberace's grand piano.

DYNAMICS OF PATTERN

Pattern not only intrigues the eye and enriches the architectural surfaces, it can be more powerful than flat color in affecting the spatial quality within an interior.

FIGURE AND GROUND

Although the general expectation is that a pattern motif lies somewhere in front of the background, a motif could sink into the surface, lie behind it, or seem to pop out in front of it, depending on the colors and shapes of both the motif and the background.

Pattern Motifs

Objects in space or motifs on a surface are known as *figure*, and the surface behind them is known as *ground* or *background*. Because vision is geared to seeing objects, pattern motifs usually stand out more prominently than the backgrounds that surround them.

Some of the calculations the brain makes in perceiving the environment have to do with locating an object in space and in relation to other objects. The same calculations are made when the eye is presented with figures or motifs or a plane surface.

- Figure is tangible and therefore easier to see than background, and is usually seen in front of background.
- Background travels behind motifs, extending to the edge of the field and, by implication, beyond it—possibly to infinity.
- Background surrounds, whereas figure is surrounded.
- Where two figures overlap, one is seen in front and the other behind.
- A spot with convex edges will seem to lie in front of its background, whereas one with concave edges may be perceived as a hole (Arnheim, 1954, p. 185).
- A shape that resembles a recognizable object is likely to be regarded as figure, irrespective of any of the preceding.

Pattern motifs often appear to lie somewhere between a fraction of an inch to several inches in front of the background, but color relationships and perspective techniques can minimize or exaggerate this separation.

- Receding background color can be exaggerated by contrast with an advancing color motif, and can make the motif more prominent.
- Where motif and background are of the same value, their separation is indistinct, and they may appear to lie at the same depth from the viewer.
- Where a receding color motif is seen against a more advancing color background, the motif can appear to lie at the same level as the surface or even behind it, unless a perspective technique brings it forward.
- Advancing color may appear to lie behind dark or neutral motifs, such as when the sunset is seen through the trees or when a pattern motif is seen through bars.
- Shading and molding can make a figure appear three-dimensional, thereby separating it from its background.
- Gradual, sequential change in form, shape, or any dimension of color is perceived as movement.
- Color contrasts and hard edges of shapes disrupt the surface by implying different viewing distances.

Subdivision of a Bounded Area

A bounded area, whether enclosed within a picture frame or defined by an architectural break, may be subdivided into any number of parts. Subdivision into large and small areas is likely to be interpreted as a figure–ground relationship, with the smaller areas seen as figure. Simple proportions, such as halves or thirds, do not read as figure and ground, nor do jigsaw puzzle pieces, and a half-and-half distribution of space is ambiguous.

2.6 DEPTH IN A TWO-COLOR PATTERN

Create a two-color pattern suitable for an interior wall or floor surface. Make three versions of it that will make the motifs appear:

a. in front of the surface,
b. at the same level as the surface, and
c. behind the surface.

(See Chapter 3.)

2.7 FIGURE–GROUND RELATIONSHIPS

Using two-color combinations:

a. Create a design in which one color appears as figure and another as ground.
b. Using the same design and colors, reverse the colors.
c. Create a design in which each color appears as both figure and ground.
d. Create an ambiguous design in which the motifs could be read as either figure or ground.

Do these designs maintain the flatness of the surface, or do they disrupt it? What makes a design suitable for a wall surface? A floor surface?

THE ILLUSION OF OVERLAPPING AND TRANSPARENCY

Transparency and overlapping create the illusion of depth on a plane surface. Whether motifs are transparent or opaque, a front-behind relationship is established. Notice the shadows and shading in Color Art 15. Because yellow and blue are complements, they neutralize one another when intermixed. Yellow is dominant in the yellow objects, and blue is dominant in the blue background.

Where two transparent films are superimposed, the complete shape of each remains visible. The overlapping films are known as the *parent shapes,* and the area of overlap is known as the *descendant* shape. The relative back–front relationship between parent and descendant shapes is indicated by the color of the descendant shape (Albers, 1963, pp. 24–26).

- Whichever parent shape color is dominant in the color of the descendant shape, that parent shape will appear to lie in front of the other.
- If two parent films are the same color, the area of overlap appears darker, because less light filters through it.
- Where more than two parent films of different colors overlap, intermixtures of these colors will appear in the areas of overlap.

The illusion of overlapping transparent colored films on a flat surface can be created using paints or colored papers (Albers, 1963, pp. 24–26. The previous effects are realistic, but interesting and unusual effects can be created by reversing the colors.

2.8 THE ILLUSION OF TRANSPARENCY USING COLORED PAPERS

a. *Select two different colors to be the parent shapes.*
b. *Select colors in intervals of one-fourth, one-half, and three-fourths of the visual distance between them. These colors are to be the descendant shapes.*
c. *Create a composition in which the two parent color shapes overlap, with the descendant color shapes in the areas of overlap defining the distances between the two parent color shapes and themselves. Remember that the parent shapes must remain visible in the areas of overlap.*

Where are the parent shapes located in depth relative to one another? Where are the descendant shapes located?

2.9

Repeat this experiment using different hue relationships and neutrals.

a. *To identify the path between complementary or contrasting hues, plot a straight line across the color circle or color solid through lower values and saturation levels.*
b. *Adjacent hues may be taken from either the high saturation hues on the perimeter of the color circle or the lower value or lower saturation hues within the hue circle.*
c. *Neutral colors may be taken from the grays.*

WALLPAPER AND ILLUSION

Wallpaper is often a source of enrichment in the interior and is of particular interest because of its prominence and because it is viewed frontally. Pattern on wall and floor surfaces affects the dynamics of both the surface on which it occurs and the space within the enclosure. Almost any patterned wall assumes greater importance than a wall of the same or similar solid color, and is generally expected to be more advancing.

So what should you consider when choosing pattern for interior use?

Complexity

The eye craves variety, stimulation, and challenge, boredom being an intolerable state. The search for the "variable, the contrasting, and the least expected" is an essential human characteristic. Engagement of the perceptual capacities provides pleasure, and is inherent in the aesthetic experience (Fiske and Maddi, 1961, p. 55).

Pattern is certainly not the only means to visual variety and stimulation, but the enrichment of interior surfaces and fabrics is universal and can be a source of enjoyment. Pattern is intended to delight and intrigue the eye, to create illusion, to stimulate fantasy and imagination, to amuse, to make a statement or, perhaps, to relieve the monotony of an otherwise uneventful interior.

Pattern choices range from simple, undemanding, and familiar motifs in quiet tints to tremendously intricate designs, sometimes with interchangeable figure and ground relationships, complex geometry (Color Art 17), and unexpected color relationships. Some patterns are ambiguous, challenging you to decide where on the surface the configurations lie or, perhaps, what they are—in other words, to "make sense" out of them. And sometimes deceptively simple configurations confront the eye with interesting mathematical relationships or proportions.

Illusion of Movement

Much of the energy that pattern introduces into an interior derives from implied movement, the question being how much and what kind of movement is desirable.

A line is like an arrow traveling through space and leading the eye along its path; a row of motifs is a dotted line that articulates movement from here to there. Where motif units are in alignment and in even geometrical distribution over the surface, movement in any one direction is balanced by movement in the opposite direction. Such a pattern is static, going nowhere, and because of its stability is a popular configuration for interior backgrounds. If the structural lines are not parallel with pattern lines, the deviation is emphasisized.

Spots lead the eye to jump from one to another, and a pattern may be deemed "spotty" if motif units are prominent and disconnected. Where motifs are tiny and close together, they may appear as texture or speckles when viewed from across the room. An allover pattern that is continuous over the surface and in which the repeats are difficult to identify can give the impression of surface continuity in all directions.

Shapes convey energy by *gesturing*. Stripes *go* up and down or sideways—or diagonally, as if to exit through an upper corner; a plaid *goes* both up and down and sideways, thereby stabilizing itself. Some shapes *radiate* outward from a center, vines *intertwine*, squares *sit* solidly on their bases or *poise* unstably on corners, or appear to *fall*. Circles can *roll* like balls or *float* like bubbles. The petals of a tulip *curve* to form a cup, and their leaves *point* upward. The shapes of both the figure and the ground *do* something.

If there is too much movement, too much contrast, too much depth, you may say that the pattern is too *busy*.

Illusion of Depth

Only a solid color surface is flat—even a line may be perceived to either lie on top of a surface or cut into it. Pattern, therefore, creates the illusion of some degree of depth and distance on a plane surface.

Part of the game is deciding at what depth motifs lie in relation to each other and the background. A "good" wallpaper pattern is generally expected to provide enrichment and intrigue the eye while at the same time maintaining the integrity of the flat surface—to "stay on the wall." Pattern can be intricate and convey the illusion of considerable depth, yet still maintain surface integrity. When pattern motifs are said to "jump out at you," it is because they violate surface integrity.

The scenic mural differs from flat pattern in that it is intended to create the illusion of depth and distance, possibly extending to infinity. The ultimate question is how the illusion of depth in wallpaper pattern might affect the spacial quality of an interior.

Light, shade, and shadow on images gives them three-dimensional characteristics. In Color Art 18 molding makes the design appear three dimensional and sets it out from the background. Despite the receding color of the motif and the advancing color of the background, the motif is perceived to lie in front of its background. The continuity of the motif and its perceived three-dimensional quality are stronger cues than the color dynamics. Shadows behind the motif place it a distance in front of the surface, and overlapping and transparency articulate depth (Color Art 19) .

Such techniques challenge the presumption of flatness, but there are no rules—the artistry of the designer determines the quality of the design.

Scale

It is easier to assess the scale of wallpaper pattern on the wall than in the wallpaper book. Small scale pattern may be effective for small rooms or for clothing, but in larger rooms where viewing distance is greater, small pattern may get lost or appear as texture.

Conversely, motifs can be too obtrusive or too large or perhaps too realistic to fit comfortably within an enclosure. It is possible to fill a room so full of pattern that there is little breathing space.

So what is "good" pattern at architectural scale, pattern compatible with large open spaces? Handsome designs with mural or supergraphic proportions are available, patterns designed with large architectural planes in mind. For example, Le Corbusier's design, "Mauer", Color Art 20, is a large module that can be assembled in a variety of ways, even horizontally.

Motif Content

Motifs may consist of polka dots, floral designs, Scottie dogs, the Mona Lisa, ships, abstracted figures, geometry, or just about anything else. No image is immune from being translated into wallpaper.

How "interesting" should motifs be in order to qualify as "good" wallpaper? Would you wish to live with Washington Crossing the Delaware repeated endlessly over a wall surface? Or Warhol's Marilyn Monroe watching you from hundreds of repetitions? Or how about an inconsequential "sprig print"? On a scale ranging between overkill and trivial, you might find trivial winning out in popularity.

Meanings attributed to wallpaper designs are discussed in Chapter 10. Meanings are more powerful than the dynamic qualities of a pattern in determining its appropriateness for a given use.

The essential fact of wallpaper, however, is that it is intended to be *background*, the scenic mural and the realistic motif notwithstanding. Wallpaper is a special type of art, but it is not a painting.

Inadvertent Images.

Gestalt is the brain's effort to make sense out of visual information by searching for recognizable images, and is sometimes referred to as the "Ah ha!" phenomenon. One of the most powerful images in human experience is the face, and if any elements of a pattern can be construed to suggest a human face, a face is what you will see. Once you see the face in the wallpaper, you will never be able to dismiss it (Color Art 21).

Sexual images are also powerful. Illusory anatomical characteristics can be created and perceived below the level of awareness of either the designer or the viewer. These and other inadvertent images, however, have a way of becoming evident and permanently engraved on the awareness.

It is good to scrutinize a pattern from some distance in order to identify such images.

FLOOR PATTERN

The integrity of the flat surface is even more important for floor surfaces than for walls, because floors get walked on. Although floor pattern can provide rich visual variety in the interior, it should appear flat as well as be flat.

Surface disruption created by exaggerated geometry or overly realistic motifs can be threatening for those with poor eyesight or for those who are not sure-

footed. If the rose on the carpet seems so real that you feel constrained to walk around it, or if the geometric pattern threatens a sprained ankle, the flatness of the surface is being violated.

A continuous floor treatment throughout a house or an interior complex can be a unifying element, but a huge expanse of uninterrupted floor surface can be as inviting as the Sahara desert. Color changes and pattern along with furnishings and architectural breaks subdivide the space, define functional areas and traffic paths, create visual interest, and relate the surface to the human dimension.

2.10 FLOOR PATTERN

Create two floor patterns:

a. one to trip the unwary, and
b. one to embellish the surface with a pattern appropriate for a designated use, yet maintain surface flatness.

CEILING PATTERN

Historically, heavily ornamented ceilings have lent importance to interiors and related large rooms to human scale. A glance at a Renaissance castle, an Adam interior (Color Art 11), or a mosque, and you may quickly conclude that ceilings then and there were of much greater importance than in contemporary buildings here and now. Consider, for example, Adam Hall shown in Color Art 11. Strongly influenced by classical Roman prototypes, Robert Adam's concept of design during the 1790s was based on delicacy and refinement. The light blue and white are spatially expansive. The overall statement is one of elegance, refinement, and grandeur but without ostentation. Of course, current building costs virtually prohibit carved plaster and gilt moldings and elaborate mosaics. Color Art 4 shows elegant use of ceiling color and design.

The ceiling design in Color Art 10 with its dark color is the dominant design element of the room. The ceiling height and ample space of the enclosure comfortably support the visual weight. The rounded cornice serves as a transition between wall and ceiling, modifying the boxlike rectangularity of the room. Ceiling interest often centers around the light fixture.

Ceilings comprise a very large percentage of the interior visual field. They are most frequently considered background, most frequently rendered in white or a tint, and seldom embellished. They seem to be the neglected stepchild of interior design. Where ceilings become a concern, ways of making them more interesting can be devised.

3 DEPTH CUES, LEGIBILITY, AND ILLUSION

As dynamic as hue can be in conveying depth and distance and defining objects, it is not the primary information on which you rely to recognize things in the environment and get where you want to go. For this you rely on the *brightness differences* that enable you to identify and locate objects, detect movement, and see where you are going.

Depth cues enable you to read the visual environment. These can be represented in a black-and-white drawing, photograph, or movie. They can also be manipulated in the visual world as well as in a representation of it.

THE VISUAL WORLD VERSUS THE VISUAL FIELD

THE VISUAL WORLD

The visual world is the stable, unbounded, continuous, three-dimensional environment that is subject to the force of gravity and that surrounds you and through which you move (Gibson, 1966, p. 253). It extends in front of, behind, above, beneath, and to either side of you, and whether you look to the right or left, up or down, or straight ahead, you are looking into depth. It is an environment of real spaces and real surfaces and objects with edges, texture, and color. It is illuminated and casts shadows. You experience it from within as a participant observer (Gibson, 1979, p. 206).

One sees the environment not just with the eyes but the eyes in the head on the shoulders of a body that gets about. We look at details with the eyes, but we also look around with the mobile head, and we go-and-look with the mobile body. (Gibson, 1979, p. 222)

THE VISUAL FIELD

The Field View of the Visual World

Although the room around you is a visual world, what you see if you look straight in front of you is a *visual field.* If you should take a photograph of what you see, the picture you would get is a *field view.* Color Art 23 depicts the visual field of a man descending a staircase. The viewer is made aware of the precarious nature of the trip. (see also Color Art 24*A* and 24*B*)

A field view of the world is, technically, what you can see with one eye and from a stationary viewing position. As far as the designer is concerned, it is what you see from a fixed viewing position, a static view of the world in which the edges of things do not move against their backgrounds. It is a sample of the environment, a bounded area, which you experience as an outside observer (Gibson, 1966, pp. 253–254).

Store displays and stage sets are primarily visual fields. Although they have some depth and may be viewed from a limited number of vantage points, they are looked at from outside themselves, rather than being experienced from within. By contrast, model rooms that you can walk through are experienced from within.

Indeed, the visual world and the visual field are intricately interrelated, and are often dealt with as two aspects of the same thing. Much can be learned about visual world space through visual field observations and experiments.

The Visual Field and Design Communication

Whether you are a design student or a design professional, you deal directly with representations of the visual world, such as models, photographs, perspective drawings and interior renderings, plan views, television and computer screens, or movies. All of these are flat—they only symbolize or stand for the three-dimensional reality they represent.

It is surprisingly easy to be seduced into believing that the drawing is the design, the end product of one's design efforts. Schools are usually equipped to deal only with design symbols, and symbolic representations are what designers think with, what gets presented to a client, and what gets published.

Of all the devices for visualizing interior space, short of the real thing or a full-scale mock-up, the architectural scale model is probably the most effective. When viewed from outside itself, it is seen as an object, but by positioning the eye at an opening the interior can be viewed from close range, thereby creating the sensation of being inside. Computer-based virtual reality may some day provide a three-dimensional world view within which students can maneuver, but as of this writing it is beyond the budgets of most educational programs.

Although architects and interior designers are concerned with the three-dimensional world of architecture, planning is usually done on a two-dimensional format. Representations are indispensable to the planning and visualization processes, particularly where form and function are concerned. Drawings, the written language of design communication, make it possible to identify and deal with design issues. The trap lies in believing that these can accurately represent surface color as it is experienced from within the architectural enclosure.

Actually, the colors, objects, and surfaces of an interior enclosure are experienced quite differently from a colored representation of that interior.

DEPTH VISION

The three-dimensional architectural interior is a bounded visual world that can comprise your total visual field. Depth vision enables you to see where the boundaries of a room are and to experience its scale and proportions. Depth vision enables you to see the forms of the furnishings within it and discern where they are in relation to yourself and each other. As you move through the space, you see things move against their backgrounds. A furnished room can seem larger than an empty room because objects in it define the space.

Without depth vision things would appear as flat shapes, and the landscape would look like so much wallpaper. Without depth vision you would not be able to distinguish objects from their backgrounds and navigate yourself among them. You have become so adept at determining what things are and where they are located, that you do it automatically and unconsciously.

As you grow older legible environments become increasingly important, as changes occur in vision that affect the ability of the elderly to relate to the environment. Farsightedness increases and depth perception declines. There is also increased sensitivity to glare and a longer time required to recover from the afterimage effects of bright light (Carter, 1982, pp. 121–129).

BRIGHTNESS

Because the visual world is structured by brightness contrast, you can see what things are, where they are located, whether or not they move, and get where you want to go without bumping into things. Presumably, a person with impaired hue vision would see the environment the way it appears in a black-and-white movie or photograph—all the information required for navigating through the visual world is adequately provided.

DEPTH CUES

Depth cues, the indicators by which we read form and spatial information, are visible only as brightness differences. Depth cues enable you to see objects, distinguish them from their backgrounds, judge distances, and see where you are going—in other words, to read the environment.

Until the cues by which you read depth are brought to your attention, you may be totally unaware of how you see the world and maneuver yourself through it, or how an interior could be made visually more interesting. You may not appreciate the need for environment legibility among people with impaired vision.

The following indicators of depth enable you to orient yourself in the environment, see objects, and navigate your way around them:

- convergence of plane surfaces,
- texture and pattern gradient,
- vertical location in the visual field,
- overlapping objects and the movement of edges against their backgrounds,
- diminishing size of objects with distance,
- movement gradient,
- object deformation gradient, and
- the use of color to simulate distance (aerial perspective).

DEPTH CUES AND ILLUSION

Depth cues can be manipulated in the environment as well as in a drawing. Stage settings routinely distort perspective cues in order to create the illusion of depth, and showroom photographers are accustomed to arranging furniture out of alignment in order to enhance the illusion of depth in a photograph. Depth cues can be emphasized, exaggerated, minimized, eliminated, distorted, or otherwise manipulated. An ingenious designer can manipulate both color and depth cues to enhance environment legibility and create illusion.

Illusion plays to our unconscious assumptions, to what we take for granted. Illusion can and should be so subtle that the viewer is unaware of any tricks.

ARCHITECTURAL PLANES

Interior space, by and large, is defined by parallel and perpendicular planes joined at right angles—walls, ceilings, and floors—although diagonal or curved walls, ramps, vaulted ceilings, domes, and unexpected construction features can also be found.

In rectangular or square rooms you experience architectural surfaces as either frontal or depth planes, depending on your orientation. *Frontal planes* appear rectangular or possibly square, whereas *depth planes* appear wedge shaped or foreshortened as they recede. Because you experience frontal and depth planes quite differently, your initial view on entering a room and your various orientations once inside are important design considerations.

FRONTAL PLANES

An interior plane viewed frontally converges toward the horizon on your left and right so gradually as to be imperceptible, and all points on the surface appear to be very nearly the same distance from the viewer. On an extremely long wall viewed frontally at midpoint and from close range, the convergence may be more noticeable.

One wall at a time may be viewed frontally. If the entrance into a room is through the center of a wall, your initial view will be a frontal view of the opposite wall, making it at least momentarily the most prominent surface in your visual field. If you are passing through a reception area, this may be the only interior surface of which you are aware.

A wall experienced frontally invites attention and may be an appropriate location for a painting, mural, or supergraphic, for rich or sensuous texture or pattern, or for an important object, such as a royal throne or a receptionist's desk.

DEPTH PLANES

A wall viewed obliquely is seen as a foreshortened depth plane. If the entrance to a room is near a corner, all walls will appear initially as depth planes. Floors and ceilings are always seen as depth planes unless viewed from the perspective of a bird's or worm's eye and from a central position directly above or below. A painting on a wall viewed at an acute angle will not be seen.

The "speed" at which a depth plane moves away from you is determined by your viewing angle. The closer you are to an end, the greater the foreshortening or convergence and the more quickly it appears to recede.

ARCHITECTURAL PLANES AND ILLUSION

Because of their long depth planes, corridors, such as airports, and large rooms, such as auditoriums and other cavernous interior spaces, are prime candidates for illusion. So are cramped spaces. Both color and depth cues influence the perception of depth of interior surfaces, and these, in turn, affect the perceived size and proportions of an enclosure.

Illusion can be put to practical advantage by visually shortening long corridors or giving huge spaces the appearance of more human scale. It must be remembered, however, that corridors and long walls are usually experienced from both ends; to make either appear shorter from one end is likely to increase apparent length when viewed from the opposite end (Color Art 29*A–C*).

Both structure and surface treatments can be altered.

DISTORTION OF THE STRUCTURE

Depth planes can be altered structurally to maximize or minimize their normal foreshortening. Sloping ceilings, ramps, or walls that are not parallel or a staircase that differs in width at bottom and top can create the appearance of greater or lesser depth.

DISTORTION OF PERSPECTIVE CUES BY ALTERING THE STRUCTURE

Structural planes converge more rapidly than parallel planes, exaggerating depth.

Structural planes converge more slowly than parallel planes, minimizing depth.

Robert Irwin's structure, "Multiple 1," on the wide staircase at the Musée d'Arte Moderne de la Ville de Paris uses this technique to both minimize and maximize apparent depth at the same time. Stairs within the structure progress in width from narrower at the bottom to wider at the top, while at the same time causing the stairs outside the structure to progress from wider at the bottom to narrower at the top (see Color Art 25*B*).

Rows of receding objects positioned not quite parallel with horizontal surfaces could subtly exaggerate or minimize the effect of convergence (Color Art 25*D*).

An ingenious designer can find numerous ways of manipulating the structure in order to create illusion.

VISUAL DISTORTION OF THE STRUCTURE

Color can either connect or disjoin architectural planes or camouflage changes in plane, thereby skewing the appearance of the structure. For example, convergent effects can be exaggerated or minimized if the ceiling color is extended onto the wall in such a way that color edges contradict structural lines and distort the right-angle relationship between architectural planes.

Color and graphic design on interior surfaces can so drastically disrupt the structure that normal relationships of the space bounding planes are visually destroyed (Color Art 2).

SURFACE VALUE DIFFERENCES
AND THE VISUAL DISTORTION OF THE STRUCTURE

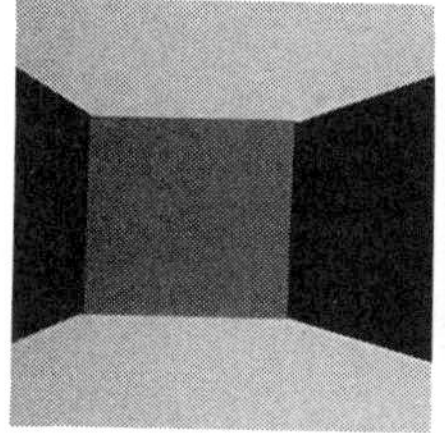

Elevation views of two end walls and a depth plane. On one end wall the dark value area is smaller than the structural plane and on one the dark value conforms to the structural plane. On the depth plane the values do not conform to the structure.

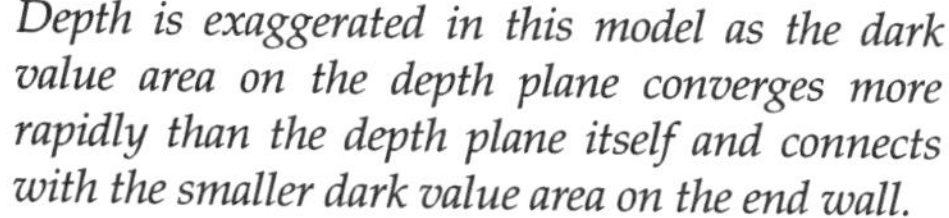

Depth is exaggerated in this model as the dark value area on the depth plane converges more rapidly than the depth plane itself and connects with the smaller dark value area on the end wall.

Depth is minimized as the dark value area on the depth plane converges more slowly than the depth plane itself.

SURFACE GRADIENT

Texture and Pattern

Here our concern is with texture and pattern on architectural surfaces—whether the texture is fine or coarse grained or very rough and large in scale, such as field stone, and whether the scale of pattern is small or large.

Texture on a receding plane normally articulates its depth more effectively than does a plain, smooth surface. Uniform texture on a surface appears coarser nearer the viewer and more compact farther away as the surface converges (Color Art 25*A*). Pattern motifs that appear large at close range gradually become smaller with distance.

Surface texture gradient: lattice work and window design, the Blue House, Korea.

NORMAL ARTICULATION OF DEPTH

Wall elevations showing evenly distributed stripes, checks, and texture.

Model showing normal convergence of evenly distributed stripes, checks, and grains of texture.

Texture and pattern gradient on a receding plane can be manipulated to exaggerate or minimize the effects of its convergence.

- The apparent depth of a receding plane can be exaggerated by using a coarser-grained texture or a larger-scaled pattern nearer the viewer and a smaller-grained texture or a smaller-scaled pattern farther away.
- The apparent depth of a receding plane can be minimized by using a finer-grained texture or a smaller-scaled pattern nearer the viewer and a coarser-grained texture or larger-scaled pattern farther away.

MINIMIZING OR EXAGGERATING DEPTH

Wall elevations showing stripes, checks, and texture graduated from larger to smaller.

Depth of the model is exaggerated where stripes, checks, or grains of texture are located at the front and become smaller at the rear.

Depth of the model is minimized where smaller stripes, checks, or grains of texture are located at the front of the model and become larger toward the rear.

On a frontal plane no gradient effects in texture or pattern are apparent over its entire surface. However, the gradient effects of a depth plane can be simulated by graduating the texture or pattern from larger to smaller over its surface.

Rough-grained surfaces disperse light, and under certain lighting conditions this dispersal can counter gradient effects. This could give the surface of a receding plane characteristics of a frontal plane.

Value–Illumination Gradient

A vertical surface that appears uniformly colored and lighted could be assumed to be a frontal plane. Gradience of color or illumination is associated with the convergent effects of a receding plane (Color Art 29*A*). Variability in both light reflectance and illumination can be used to exaggerate or to minimize the perceived depth of a receding plane. Darkness tends to be more advancing or to "close in" on you, whereas lightness tends to be more expansive. Warm colors are perceived as advancing and cool colors as receding. Unless the values of the hues are controlled, however, you may base depth judgments on value differences rather than hue differences (Color Art 29*B* and *C*).

An architectural plane can be lighted at either end, so that from the viewer's position it can move from lighter to darker or from darker to lighter. As the plane moves away from a light source, the intensity of light on the surface diminishes and its color becomes darker. If the surface moves out of darkness into light, the light becomes brighter and its color lighter. As seen by the viewer:

- Gradation from dim lighting or darkness at close range to bright lighting farther away can exaggerate the depth of a receding plane; gradation from bright lighting at close range to dim light or darkness farther away can minimize its perceived depth.
- Gradation from dark color at close range to light color farther away can exaggerate the depth of a receding plane; gradation from light color at close range to dark color farther away can minimize its apparent depth.
- Light color dimly lit or dark color brightly lit could negate the dynamic potential of both color and light.

Aerial Perspective and Color Gradient

Outdoors on a foggy day only near objects are distinct, whereas objects in the distance are seen through increasingly dense fog—the denser the fog, the less distinct forms and colors become. Distant mountains appear bluish because their image is filtered through the atmosphere. Bluishness and mistiness characterize aerial perspective and can be simulated indoors by either:

- the use of distinct, clear colors on near objects and surfaces and grayed, paler, or bluish colors on those farther away, or
- a mural on an end wall in which foreground objects are shown with distinct shapes and clear colors, but in the distance the forms become less and less distinct and their colors become lighter, grayer, and bluer.

In an interior the use of soft, bluish colors on near objects and surfaces and clear, distinct colors on those farther away could counter the illusion of distance.

REFLECTIVE SURFACES

To a greater or lesser degree, every surface in an interior enclosure reflects light and color. A mirror reflects all of the images, light, and color falling on it, and a glossy surface somewhat less.

One mirrored wall in a room visually doubles the space and the things, people, activity, and color in the enclosure (Color Art 12), whereas mirrors reflecting into each other from several surfaces can create a dizzying and infinite multiplication of images. Polished floors or other reflective surfaces pick up and reflect images and colors from the surroundings, contributing significantly to the illusion of depth and imparting considerable liveliness to the enclosure. Such reflections, like pattern, belong to the surface and converge as the surface converges.

OVERLAPPING PLANES

Solid Planes

As overlapping architectural planes are viewed obliquely, the eye can calculate the distances between them (Color Art 6, 9, and 26). They may be separated by brightness differences and perhaps by differences in hue. Overlapping also occurs wherever a projecting corner is seen against a wall behind it. Not only do overlapping planes enable you to estimate depth, but as you move the relationships change. The movement of a surface or a corner against a background as you walk past it is a powerful depth cue.

Transparent Planes

Transparent film between you and what lies behind it can be an effective cue for gauging depth. It enables the eye to gauge:

- the distance between yourself and the film,
- the distance between the film and what is behind it, and
- the distance between the films if there are two or more layers of transparent film.

A colored transparent plane imparts its color to what is seen through it, and as the colors of two or more overlapping transparent planes become intermixed, additional depth information is provided.

A translucent plane implies that space and light exist behind it. Consider Color Art 28. The sculptural use of light and transparent materials serves as a focal point and articulates the open space of the three-story lobby of the corporate headquarters of the First Union Bank.

3.1 SURFACE TREATMENTS AND THE ILLUSION OF DEPTH IN A CORRIDOR MODEL

Create two identical models of a hotel corridor. One of the vertical walls may be omitted to admit light. If the model is viewed as though along the edge of the missing panel, that wall will be perceived as a plane seen on end. The design can emphasize any technique or combination of techniques for altering the appearance of depth. Using only surface treatments, alter the appearance of depth in the two models:

a. In one model shorten the apparent visual depth,
b. In the other model lengthen the apparent visual depth.

Display the two models together for comparison.

INTERIOR OBJECTS AND ILLUSION

Both the enclosure and the objects within it derive their scale from one another, and objects define the space within the enclosure as surely as do the space-bounding architectural surfaces. Visual depth is calculated by comparing the apparent sizes of near and far objects. The location of objects depends on near–far, side-by-side, above–below, and behind-in-front comparisons.

DIMINISHING SIZE WITH DISTANCE

If two chairs in a room are the same size, one closer to you and the other farther away, the closer chair is larger in your visual field and the one farther away is smaller. Because of size constancy, however, you know that they are the same size, and you are familiar with the fact of diminishing size with distance. You can, therefore, make a reasonable calculation of the relative distance between them.

Because you assume that objects diminish in size with distance, the placement of two objects, one smaller and one larger, one nearer and one farther away, could alter your perception of their distances and the depth of the enclosure.

- If the larger cube were nearer to you and the smaller one were farther away, you could assume greater distance between them, and the depth of the enclosure would appear to be greater.
- If the smaller cube were nearer to you and the larger one farther away, you could assume less distance between them, and the depth of the enclosure would be minimized.

In a Japanese garden tall trees were planted nearer the house and smaller trees farther away in order to promote the illusion of depth (Lang, 1987, p. 226).

THE RELATIVE SCALE OF OBJECTS AND INTERIOR SPACE AND THE PERCEPTION OF DEPTH

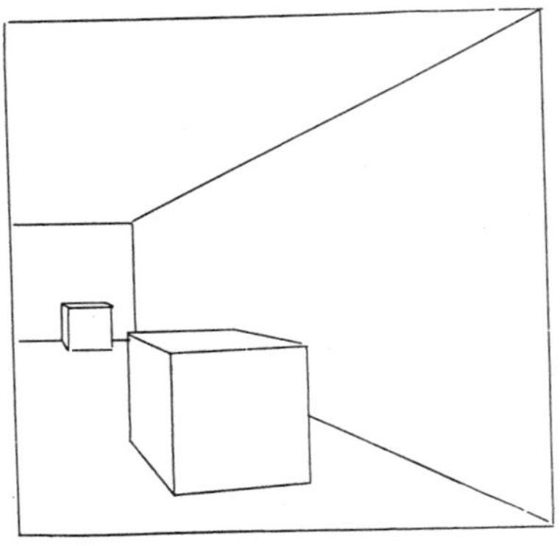

Normal articulation of depth occurs when cubes of the same size are positioned at different distances from the viewer.

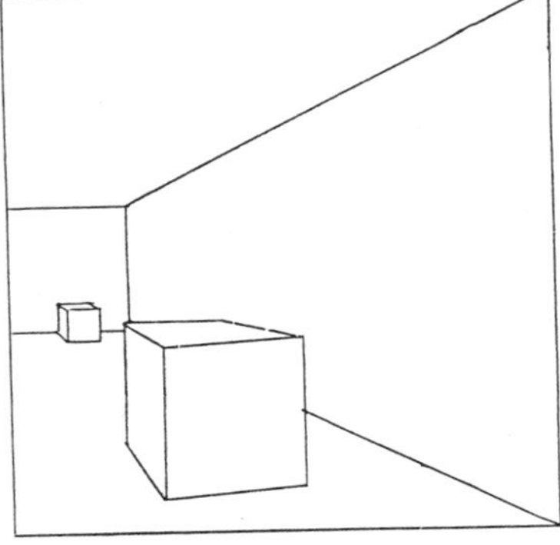

Depth is exaggerated when a larger cube is located nearer the viewer and a smaller cube is farther away.

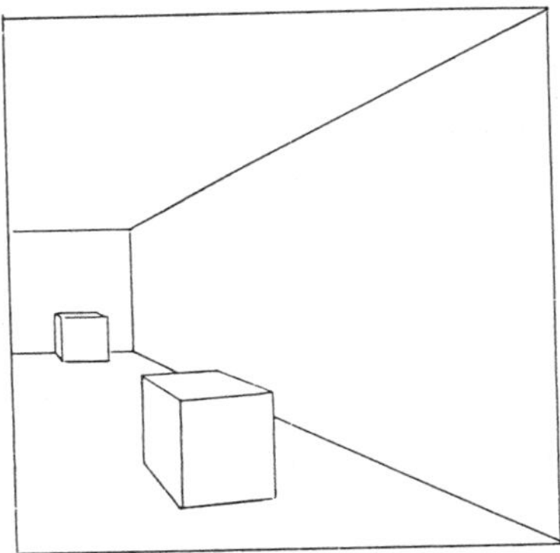

Depth is minimized when a smaller cube is located nearer the viewer and a larger cube is farther away.

VERTICAL LOCATION IN THE VISUAL FIELD

Because the ground underfoot appears to rise on its way toward the horizon, objects on the ground appear to rise with the ground. A figure placed above another in a painting is perceived to be located farther away than one below it. Elevating an object also increases its importance as well as its distance.

Upward location with distance is a powerful indicator of depth, a more powerful cue perhaps than diminishing size. It has been widely used in Egyptian, Oriental, and medieval paintings, as well as in the paraline drawings used extensively by designers. The mural shown in Color Art 30 is not only a work of art, it extends the visual space by means of upward location of motifs in the visual field.

If the floor at the far end of a large enclosure were raised by a few steps, would this subtly result in objects placed there appearing somewhat farther away than if the floor remained level? Would lowering the floor by a few steps subtly decrease the effect of distance?

If upward or downward location in the eye of the beholder has the presumed effect, an auditorium floor that slopes downward toward the stage could be assumed to make people and furniture on the stage appear closer to the audience. As seen by those on stage, the size of the auditorium and the audience would appear more expansive.

MOVEMENT

The perception of movement, like the perception of depth, is independent of hue perception. Different kinds of movement serve to articulate interior space: You can move, things in the enclosure can move, or movement can be implied or fantasized.

You can physically wend your way through the space, you can trace a path with your eye, or you can make the trip in fantasy with your eyes closed. However the movement is experienced, it should be pleasurable.

Movement of the Observer

Movement can bring life to an interior and make it more interesting. Movement of your own body through an interior is probably your most effective source of information about the scale and arrangement of the space. You have developed a vocabulary of spatial volume experiences by moving yourself from here to there through interior spaces and around furnishings and up and down stairs. Previous experiences making depth and distance judgments enable you to visualize and deal with spaces vicariously.

Overlapping is a powerful cue as to where things are in relation to each other. If you see a chair in front of a table in front of a window, you intuitively gauge their relative sizes, how far they are from you, the distances between them, and how they relate to the spatial boundaries. You can get a better sense of their relative sizes and distances, however, by walking past them and observing how they move against one another and the background. Near objects move more quickly against their backgrounds, and objects farther away move more slowly. Gibson identifies this as the *gradient of motion* (Gibson, 1950, pp. 118–119).

Although viewing distances inside a room cannot compare with vistas seen from a passing train, walking through interior spaces and past furnishings, columns, and other architectural features not only enables you to judge depth and distance, it also enlivens the scene. Walking past a transparent or translucent screen, a lacy iron fence, or a see-through wall amplifies movement and lends interest to the trip. The iron grillwork shown in Color Art 31 serves as a transparent screen that enables the eye to gauge distances in front and behind it. Further depth information is provided by the changing position of objects behind the screen as you move past it.

Freestanding objects such as posts, tall sculpture or plants, furniture, and chandeliers also serve the same purpose (Color Art 26, 14, and 28). Their relative positions change as you walk past them. Furniture and other objects placed tightly against the wall are static, adding nothing to the dynamic quality of a room.

The form of an object also changes as you view it from changing positions. Gibson defines this as the *gradient of deformation* (Gibson, 1950, p. 118). Walking past a chair, you see first a front view, a corner view, and then a side view—same object, different shapes. Symmetrical shapes such as chandeliers or columns appear the same from any direction.

Movement of the Object

Although the furnishings in an interior are generally stationary, people and pets do move through the space, and some objects are put there because they move.

Someone walking toward you or away from you measures off distance more effectively than someone standing still. If you watch a person walk behind a stationary object, climb stairs, disappear down a hall, and emerge somewhere else, his or her changing locations relative to the stationary architecture provide significant depth information. Such movement also makes the building more interesting. One reason that box-type spaces are visually boring is that, once inside them, there is nowhere for the eye or the imagination to go.

Although fountains, mobiles, and electric fans move, they have a fixed point of attachment and are only effective in defining depth in the same way as stationary objects. However, in large complex interior spaces, a fountain, a large clock, or some other object of focal interest can be a landmark, whose very presence helps to define the space.

Implied Movement

Brilliant and apparently moving neon lights overhead dominate the concourse at O'Hare Airport in Chicago. As they change from one hue to another across the huge expanse of ceiling, their implied movement is either coming toward you or going away from you, depending on the direction in which you happen to be traveling. The sense of movement is emphasized as everyone in the space is in motion. Not only do these lights entertain and amuse and distract your attention from the long trek ahead, they also shorten the visual distance to be traversed, especially when they are moving toward you. The scale of the lights is related to the

3.2 A SPACE FRAME

Envision a block of space 12″x 12″x 12″ in front of you, which is indistinguishable from the space in the rest of the room. Define the dimensions of this cube and articulate the volume of space within this block, not merely its outer boundaries. This requires putting something into it. Make the structure self-supporting so that it can be viewed from every angle.

One of the following elements should be dominant in the composition although other elements may be used as well:

Lines
Planes
Solid forms
Transparent or opaque materials
Color

How much or how little solid material is necessary to define this designated volume of space? Compare this structure with other structures. Which have the greatest apparent depth or size when viewed from all sides? How do you account for the apparent differences in size? Which are the most interesting and why?

enormous scale of the corridor, and because they occupy so much visual space, they impart to the interior a more human scale.

Gradient can often be as effective as a directional arrow in directing your movement, whether it be surface gradient or gradient in illumination, color, texture, line, form, or structural elements.

Implied movement has characterized much optical and kinetic art. A number of techniques for creating apparent change in objects or surfaces as you move include the following (Barrett, 1971):

- patterns produced by overlapping mesh screens,
- moiré effects produced by lines or rods overlapping at slightly different angles, and
- colored slats in front of a striped colored background producing shifting color effects as you move by them.

3.3 ARTICULATING THE SPACE WITHIN AN INTERIOR MODEL

In an interior model of your own choosing, place furnishings and, if you wish, architectural features. Your purpose is to make the volume of the enclosed space interesting, while taking into account space for people and activities.

This entails interaction between:

a. the space-bounding surfaces,
b. the space within the enclosure, and
c. the objects within the enclosure.

Apply color to the surfaces and objects. Furniture may be represented by cubes, balls, or other abstract forms.

What difference does color make in the perceived volume of enclosed space? In the size, distance, and balance of objects? What difference would movement make?

3.4 AN ENCLOSURE TO TRIP THE UNWARY

Design an interior space that would appear "normal" in every way but would be as illegible and illusory as possible. Both color and perspective cues can be manipulated to mislead the viewer and create confusion.

4 SEEING COLOR AND WHAT IS COLORED

Having seen the colored environment all of your life, would you believe that your eye does not see it? Light reflected from surfaces triggers only electrochemical responses in the eye. These nerve impulses are translated into meaningful sense at higher levels within the optical system and the brain, which has access to memory by means of an unbelievably complex network of interacting neurons. Only then does seeing take place.

Like the tree that falls silently in the forest where there is no ear to hear it, color does not exist until it is seen. *Color is a perception that occurs only inside your brain.*

The business of designers is that of creating visual experiences. By understanding something about how we see, you may be able to take advantage of knowing that every stage in the processing of visual information in some way affects how we see color and what is colored, and can be subject to design intervention.

WHAT IS SEEING?

The purpose of vision is to *see objects and locate them in space.* This involves being able to distinguish things from their backgrounds, primarily by means of brightness differences, hue playing an auxiliary role.

Seeing is at every stage a complex decision-making process. Seeing is a matter of:

- sorting out the jumble of light rays that enter the eye,
- processing the visual information through many stages,
- synthesizing this information with that from other senses and with memories of previous experiences and emotions,

- decoding and organizing it into meaningful sense, and
- deciding how to feel about it and what to do about it.

Each stage of the seeing process determines some aspect of your perception of the environment, and it all takes place in the flash of an instant and without your awareness. Seeing is an *unconscious process,* every aspect of which is essentially a matter of comparing and subtracting, making connections, defining, interpreting, and making judgments.

THE EYE

THE STRUCTURE OF THE EYE

Seeing begins when reflected light enters the eye and falls upon the retina, a thin, transparent sheet of tissue at the back of the eye that is sensitive to light.

The pupil, the small, round, black opening in the center of the iris, the colored part of the eye, regulates the amount of light entering the eye. In bright light the pupil contracts, reducing the amount of light that enters the eye, and in darkness or dim light it expands to admit more light. Because of your pupil's adaptability, you can see in both quite dim light and dazzling sunlight. When you move suddenly from bright sunshine into a darkened theater, however, it may take minutes for your eye to adapt well enough to find a seat, and even coming indoors on a sunny day may require some time before you can see well. It takes longer for the eye to adjust from lighter to darker than from darker to lighter (Gerritsen, 1983, p. 53). A sudden move from darkness into bright light can be painful until your eye adjusts, such as when you wake at night and turn on the light.

Two eyes give you stereoscopic depth vision, the ability to see an object from two vantage points. This extends the breadth of your vision beyond what you could see with one eye, and is useful in judging differences between near and far and in defining objects. Depth vision is also accommodated by the ability of the lens to focus on objects at different distances.

EYE MOVEMENT AND SEEING

If the eye is fixated on a totally motionless image for a prolonged period of time, the image begins to fade and disappear. Experiencing an interior would not foster such intense gaze, because many points of visual interest stimulate eye movement, but if all surfaces were a vivid red, the color would come to appear less intense as the eye became saturated.

Vision depends on making comparisons, and comparisons require eye movement.

Different kinds of eye movement are necessary for seeing:

- Smooth motions or slow drifts when you are keeping a moving object in sight by moving either your eyes or your head.
- Fast jumps when you move your eyes from one fixed point to another, as when you read, look at a painting, scan a landscape, or watch a tennis match.
- Eye-fixation movements when you look at a work of art that requires visual involvement—the reason why some modern artists produce very large-scale works.
- Rapid oscillations or tremors of receptor cells, occurring at a frequency of 30 to 70 per second, that shift the image from fatigued cells to different receptors, thereby keeping the image from fading (Bloomer, 1976, pp.29–30).

VISION AND AGE

Infancy and Early Childhood

Although much of an infant's poor visual acuity is due to the immaturity of the brain, the retina is not fully developed until about 4 years of age (Sekuler and Blake, 1985, p. 61). Yet visual ability is developed at an astonishingly early age. From birth infants actively seek out information about their environment. By 4 to 5 months of age, they are sensitive to depth, orientation, location, and movement, and they can discriminate discrete hues of blue, green, yellow, and red (Bornstein, and Lamb, 1988, p. 185).

Seeing has to be learned. Visual deprivation in infancy can prevent the development of the visual system, and a child may never learn to see (Hubel, 1995, p. 193). Color deprivation can lead to color insensitivity later in life.

Aging

As a person becomes elderly, changes occur in the eye that affect color vision:

- Yellowing of the crystalline lens, so that what one sees resembles what a younger person would see when looking through a yellow filter, that is, a relative darkening of blue and a general bias of colors toward those of longer wavelengths.
- Increased sensitivity to glare and a longer time required to recover from the afterimage effects of bright light (Carter, 1982, pp. 121–129).

THE RETINA

The retina is the screen on which an image is cast. It is located on the back of the eye and is regarded as a specialized part of the surface of the brain that has budded out and become sensitive to light (Gregory, 1966, pp. 45–47).

MACULAR, FOVEAL, AND PERIPHERAL VISION

Parts of the retina include:

- The *macula,* a small area of the retina that you use for looking at something directly or for reading.
- The *fovea,* located at the center of the macula, with the largest concentration of receptors. Here vision is most acute, enabling you to examine fine details.
- *Peripheral vision,* the area of the retina outside the macula, less sensitive to color and more sensitive to brightness and movement.

You can examine in detail only a small area, but by scanning you can see the entire visual field in front of you. If you focus your eyes on your finger held out in front of you, you are using your macular vision, and, without moving your eyes, what you see of the surrounding area is your peripheral vision. How far can you move your other hand out to the side and still see it out of the corner of your eye? Wiggling your fingers makes them more visible. How far toward the center do you need to bring this hand before you can see its color well? What size area can you see in the most minute detail? Things that move, such as mobiles, pets, and electric fans capture the attention.

If something interesting appears in peripheral vision, that triggers the impulse to investigate it more thoroughly with macular vision. An interesting interior intrigues the viewer with objects, patterns, textures, and interesting spaces caught in peripheral vision, thereby triggering one macular inspection after another. An interior with few interesting elements worth exploring visually, where everything can be grasped in a single glance, is surely boring.

THE RECEPTOR CELLS

Photoreceptor or light-sensitive cells on the retina are known as *cones* and *rods,* and about 130 million separate messages fall on as many of these cells. Like individual tiles in a mosaic, each cell specifies the kind and level of light falling on it.

Cones and rods, themselves, do not actually "see"; their only function is to absorb wavelengths of light reflected from surfaces in the environment and to emit electrical signals when light hits them (Hubel, 1995, p. 2). Light converts photochemicals in these cells into electrical signals, the language which the brain understands (Livingston, 1988, p. 78).

Cones

Cones are hue-sensitive cells largely concentrated in the macula. Because they are so small, this is where visual acuity is sharpest. Hue sensitivity has developed in response to the visible wavelengths of the sunlight spectrum, which range from approximately 400 to 700 nanometers, or billionths of a meter. The eye is blind to wavelengths outside this range, such as ultraviolet, infrared, X-rays, or radio waves.

There are three types of cones, each maximally sensitive to a particular range of wavelengths (Livingstone, 1988, p. 78) (Color Art 33*A*):

- Shorter wavelengths activate blue and green receptors.
- Medium wavelengths activate green receptors,
- Longer wavelengths activate red receptors.

The responses of each type of cone, however, are very broad and overlap considerably. Color is the consequence of unequal stimulation of the three types of cones (Hubel, 1995, p. 166).

Cones are sensitive to brightness as well as hue, and they gather all of the information required to identify objects and surfaces and locate them in space.

Rods

Most rod cells are located on the retina outside the concentration of the hue-sensitive cones of the macula, and in the far corner of your eye you have only rod vision. Rods come into play when light is too dim to activate cone vision. They respond only to light–dark differences, and, being highly sensitive to light, they enable you to see in dim light, so that you can drive at night or find a seat in a dark theater. You cannot see colors in moonlight, even though you can see where you are going.

Peripheral vision, which is primarily rod vision, is largely insensitive to color but highly responsive to movement. From an evolutionary point of view, rod vision is the more primitive way of seeing. Movement and spots in peripheral vision trigger a reflex that makes you turn your attention to them (De Grandis, 1984, p. 74)—the same reflex that enables a frog to catch bugs.

THE COLLECTOR CELLS

The signal from each cone or rod receptor cell is passed on to a collector or ganglion cell on the retina (Color Art 33*B*). Ganglions themselves do not respond to light but process the information received from the rods and cones by generating brief electrical discharges.

About one million interconnected and richly overlapping ganglions form a receptive field on the retina, where messages from the rod and cone cells are reorganized and information is shared (Hubel, 1995, p. 43). Because there are fewer ganglions than photoreceptors, this indicates that information is being condensed (Sekuler and Blake, 1985, p. 66). So begins the sorting and processing of visual information into a more manageable form. A neural fiber from each ganglion continues through the optic nerve to higher levels of information processing.

Large Ganglion Cells and the Response to Brightness

There are two types of ganglions—large and small. They differ not only in size but in the way they process information. The vast majority of ganglions are the large or M (magnocellular) cells, which carry information about brightness contrast or dark–light differences. They simply add together all the information received from the red-, blue-, and green-sensitive cone cells without distinguishing one hue signal from another. They are, therefore, hue-blind (Livingstone, 1988, p. 78).

Large ganglion cells require spatial comparison. "White is seen only when the light from the object is less than the average amount of light coming from the surrounding regions" (Hubel, 1995, p. 173). Large ganglion cells detect quick movements of objects, whereas small ganglion cells specify the colors and fine details of those objects (Sekuler and Blake, 1994, p. 72).

SMALL GANGLION CELLS AND THE RESPONSE TO COLOR AND BRIGHTNESS

Small or P (parvocellular) ganglion cells distinguish hues from one another by comparing and subtracting information provided by the three types of cones. This is accomplished by means of:

- two opponent channels, red–green and yellow–blue, and
- one nonopponent channel that combines signals from all three types of cones and registers only brightness.

Color Art 33*B* shows how the opponent channels might be connected to the red-, blue-, and green-sensitive cones. Color Art 33*C* shows that:

- yellow for the yellow–blue channels is produced by combining signals from the red- and green-sensitive cones, and
- brightness response results from a combination of signals from both red–green and yellow–blue channels.

The ganglion cell has a center–surround structure, a circular center surrounded by a much larger ring-shaped region, and it will be either ON-center or OFF-center (Color Art 30*D*). Although it may receive information from several types of cone cells, each ganglion cell responds to only one kind of stimulus (Sekuler and Blake, 1994, pp. 71–74).

Red–green, green–red, blue–yellow and yellow–blue ganglions overlap in the receptive field that covers the central portion of the retina. They do not cancel each other out but work separately:

- An ON red–OFF green ganglion will fire in response to red light only, and an ON green–OFF red ganglion will fire in response to green light only. A red–green or a green–red ganglion cannot fire both red and green at the same time.
- An ON blue–OFF yellow ganglion will fire in response to blue light only, and and an ON yellow–OFF blue ganglion will fire in response to yellow light only. A blue–yellow or a yellow–blue ganglion cannot fire both blue and yellow at the same time.
- If red, green, blue, and yellow are all activated, white is seen; if none are activated, black is seen.

Ganglions add and subtract like a calculator. The opponent channel system provides a surprisingly efficient means for comparing light signals from the cones and for registering the entire range of visible hues in all possible values and saturation levels. Most surfaces in the environment reflect some amount of all spectral hues and vary in their brightness, and the ability of ganglions to discriminate both hue and brightness in any combination enables you to distinguish up to nine million colors (Gerritsen, 1983, p. 68)

OPPONENT CELL		OPPONENT CELL		PERCEPTION
Red	— Green	Yellow	– Blue	
+	-	-	-	Red
-	+	-	-	Green
+	+	+	-	Yellow
-	-	-	+	Blue
+	-	+	-	Orange
+	-	-	+	Magenta
-	+	-	+	Cyan
+	+	+	+	Bright
-	-	-	-	Dark

The Edge Response

The ganglion center–surround structure is an ingenious device for registering changes in the light, such as where the edge of an object separates it from its background.

When the image contains an edge, such as where two contiguous colors come together, where an object differs from its background, or where a shadow falls on a brightly lit background, there is a markedly strong response as the interconnected ganglions busily compute the differences in brightness levels on both sides of the edge. Edge contrast is maximized as comparisons are made. Raw messages received from cones are translated into information about edges and textures and, therefore, about objects (Sekuler and Blake, 1994, p. 74).

THE LATERAL GENICULATE BODIES

Information from each large M and small P ganglion cell on the retina is transmitted via its own neural fiber in the optic nerve complex to two peanut-sized clusters of neurons known as the *lateral geniculate bodies,* which lie deep within the brain. Here information is segregated into two distinct subdivisions, the parvo (P) and magno (M) systems, which serve two distinctly different purposes (Livingstone, 1988, p. 79).

THE PARVO SYSTEM

The parvo system receives information from the small P ganglion cells about both hue and brightness contrast. It can distinguish between any two hues, such as red and green, whether there is any brightness difference between them or not.

Ordinarily, brightness differences play an important role in separating one color from another, but when two colors are the same value, the edge between them is unstable, often appearing to vibrate or waver, and shapes and forms are indistinct. A page whose print is the same value as its background is difficult if not impossible to read. A wallpaper design in two hues of the same value would appear perfectly flat and its motifs indistinct.

Because the parvo system has a slow time response and high resolution, it is probably important for seeing stationary objects in great detail (Livingstone, 1988, p. 82).

THE MAGNO SYSTEM

The magno system receives brightness contrast information from the large M ganglion cells and detects form, depth, and movement.

Although more sensitive to brightness contrast than the parvo system, it is color blind, unable to distinguish hues at any brightness level. It sees the world only in black, white, and shades of gray, as in a black-and-white photograph. The magno system sees things as a whole, so that elements that belong to a single object are grouped together. If the magno system is intact, the person with impaired hue vision can distinguish objects, make depth judgments, stay clear of an oncoming car, and navigate through the environment.

Because it has a faster time response and a greater sensitivity to movement than the parvo system, it is particularly good at detecting motion but poor at scrutinizing stationary images (Livingstone, 1988, p. 82). Hard-to-see objects can be made more visible by introducing movement.

Because brightness information is processed through both the magno and the parvo systems, this indicates the predominance of brightness over hue in vision.

CORTICAL VISUAL AREAS

FORM, DEPTH, AND COLOR SIGNALS

Information from the lateral geniculate bodies is transmitted to visual areas at the rear of the cortex, where the different visual functions rearrange themselves into three major pathways:

- One highly selective for hue and brightness but not for shape or movement.
- One selective for orientation, object and shape analysis, and movement, but not for color.
- One selective for orientation, depth, and movement.

Visual signals continue to be fed into these three pathways at still higher stages of brain function and are analyzed by:

- the color system,
- the form system, and
- the movement, location, and depth system (Livingstone, 1988, p. 85).

Ultimately, the three separate images from the three separate systems are united to create an integrated visual whole. When a red ball is being thrown toward you, you simultaneously see its roundness, its redness, and its changing position as it moves through space. When you observe an interior, you do not visually separate walls and furniture from their colors and textures, their location, or their changing shapes in your visual field as you move past them.

SEEING

Scientists do not know exactly where or how seeing takes place, but it is somewhere in your brain. The brain's function is to make sense out of the veritable deluge of detailed information that falls on the retina.

CONSTANCY

Constancy enables your brain to evaluate visual information, compare it with past visual experiences, calculate what it is expected to be, and make sense out of it. In order to do this, you must be able to see the whole environment.

You tend to see something the way you have learned that it ought to be. A door remains a rectangle whether you see it closed, ajar, or open. The table top is square, even though you see it as a trapezoid, and it maintains its up–down relationship to the earth whether you tilt your head or stand on your head. A man does not change in size as he walks away from you, becoming smaller in your field of vision. White surfaces are seen as white whether the light is bright, dim, or colored, diffuse, or patches of sunlight and shadow. "We get along in this world because we consistently and persistently disbelieve the plain evidence of our senses" (Boulding, 1966, p. 14).

Without constancy the world around you would be an unintelligible mess of unrelated bits and pieces, and nothing would make any sense.

THE BRAIN AS COMPUTER

It is said that seeing is believing; however, as Langer points out, "Not simply seeing is believing, but seeing and calculating, seeing and translating" (Langer, 1951, p. 29). Utilizing its vast network of neural connections, the brain compares, decodes, computes, organizes, eliminates the irrelevant, and converts visual information into symbols, which are what the brain thinks with. Such a feat has been equaled by only one computer—its name was Hal, and nothing has been seen of it since *2001: A Space Odyssey.*

"The essence of seeing is more a matter of the organization and interpretation of information than of light patterns on the retina" (Miller, 1971, p. 42). As your brain compares what you see with your cumulative past visual experiences, it draws conclusions and makes inferences. All of your previous experiences with interior color provide the background against which your brain can compare incoming information and make judgments.

Furthermore, seeing is instantaneous—one of the fastest responses on record—and you don't know how you do it!

5 OPTICAL INTERACTIONS AMONG COLORS

No color ever appears alone but always in the context of other color. Where two colors appear together, optical interactions occur, sometimes drastically changing the appearance of both.

An edge distinguishes an object from its background, separates one color from another, or makes a dark shadow stand out against a brightly lit patch of sunshine. We are interested in both the quality of the edge and the changes in appearance hue that occur where two colors interact.

The ability to control color interaction requires the ability to distinguish between different kinds of color differences.

MAKING FINE DISCRIMINATIONS IN COLOR

The ability to fine-tune surface color differences and samenesses is as important to the designer as the ability to tune a violin is to the violinist. As Josef Albers said, "If one is not able to distinguish between a higher tone and a lower tone, one probably should not make music" (Albers, 1963, p. 12).

Just as some musicians have an ear for pitch, some people have an eye for color. Usually, however, the designer's eye, like the musician's ear, must be trained to make fine discriminations.

SEEING COLOR DIFFERENCES AND SAMENESSES

Every color decision you will ever make involves a decision regarding its hue, its value, and its saturation. Which characteristics of a color make it advance or recede? Which characteristics make a surface appear flat or disrupted? What optical effects result from the various combinations?

If two color swatches of the same material are placed together and are identical in hue, value, and saturation, there is no difference between them and they appear as one color. But if they differ, what is the nature of that difference?

- Do they differ in hue, in value, or in saturation?
- Do they differ in only one of these dimensions, two, or all three?
- Are the differences great or small?
- How do the differences affect the edge where they are seen together?

Color expertise assumes the ability to distinguish between hue, value, and saturation—a task that can be more difficult than you might expect. Differences can be assessed only *by making comparisons between contiguous colors.*

EYE TRAINING

You can develop the ability to make fine discriminations between any two colors only by making choices yourself and studying their interactions. In Color At 34, hue, value, and saturation are dealt with as three variables, two of which are held constant, differences occuring in the third. Two colors may be: the same hue and saturation, but differ in value; the same hue and value, but differ in saturation; the same saturation and value, but are closely adjacent hues; the same saturation and value, but are strongly contrasting or complementary hues.

Hue differences, value differences, and saturation differences can be isolated and compared as to how each affects the separation of forms from their backgrounds, surface flatness or disruption, and the quality of edges.

Crisp edges separate contiguous colors of different values, as ganglions exaggerate the differences on both sides of the edge between them. Value differences distinguish forms and shapes from one another and their backgrounds, and disrupt the flatness of a surface.

Without value differences, hue and saturation differences are visible to only the parvo system, which cannot distinguish one form or shape from another. Colors that differ only in saturation separate minimally, depending on the advancing quality of the more vivid hue and the receding quality of the same hue at low saturation. Closely adjacent hues of identical value and saturation could fuse without even the suggestion of an edge between them. Where complementary or strongly contrasting hues of the same value and saturation are juxtaposed, however, the ganglions seem to go wild in their rush to intensify their differences, and the edge that separates them appears "electric."

The hexagons in Color Art 35, are based on the hue circle colors, and progress from blue in the center, through blue-green, green, yellow-green, and so on, to blue in the outer rim. Examples show progressions from lighter to darker and from darker to lighter, and similar values overall.

5.1 COLOR DIFFERENCES AND SAMENESSES

Identify color combinations with the following characteristics. The 6″× 9″ color pack colors are a good color source. Present as stripes approximately 1 inch wide to maximize the contact edge. It is good to select several pairs of each and choose the best example from among them.

a. ***Five color swatches are the same hue and saturation but differ only in value.*** *These are easy to find, but the challenge is to keep the intervals even. Look for fluting.*
b. ***Two color swatches are the same hue and value but differ only in saturation.*** *Squint your eyes very tightly to exclude everything except value. When the values are the same, the edge between the two seems to disappear as the colors fuse together. You may wish to find complementary hues and the saturation gradations between them.*
c. ***Two color swatches are the same value and saturation but are closely related adjacent hues from a small arc on the hue circle.*** *If you begin with a hue from the middle-value range, you will find more adjacent hues of similar value than if you begin with the yellows or purples. If the values are the same, you will hardly be able to see an edge. If an edge is discernible, the values are not the same.*
d. ***Two color swatches are the same value and saturation but are complementary or strongly contrasting hues.*** *Hues from the middle-value range work best—blues through greens and orange through magentas. The contact edge between complementary hues of the same value should be highly unstable—it should "vibrate" or appear "electric."*

Which combinations appear flat? Which combinations disrupt the surface?

SIMULTANEOUS CONTRAST

When the eye sees an edge, it compares the colors on both sides of it and computes and maximizes the differences. This visual phenomenon is known as *simultaneous contrast,* and it makes color "the most relative medium in art"; it "deceives continually" (Albers, 1963, p. 1).

- Light color makes dark color appear darker, and dark color makes light color appear lighter.
- Complementary colors intensify one another.
- Hues adjacent to one another on the color circle seem to "push each other apart," as their differences are maximized.
- Vivid colors make grayed colors appear grayer, and grayed colors make vivid colors appear more vivid.

EXAMPLES FROM PERCEPTION PSYCHOLOGY

The Hermann Grid

Where a white grid is seen against a black background, the white appears whiter than white and the black appears blacker than black. However, darker shadowy spots mysteriously appear at the intersections, but seem to go away when you look at them directly. The dimming effect that causes the spots at the intersections is not the illusion; the illusion is the excessive whiteness of the grid stripes against the enhanced blackness of the background (Sekuler and Blake, 1994, pp. 74–79). Similarly, on a black grid imposed on a white background, lighter spots appear at the intersections.

THE HERMANN GRID. *The grayish patches you see at the intersections are not the illusion—the illusion is the exaggerated whiteness between the black squares where white and black are closer together and the intersection is stronger.*

Mach Bands

Simultaneous contrast is also demonstrated by stripes in which color change is gradual and sequential. Although each stripe is of uniform color, at each edge the difference between the color and its neighbor is maximized; for example, a stripe appears lighter on the side next to its darker neighbor and darker on the side next to its lighter neighbor. This is evidence of ganglions at work, making comparisons, exaggerating differences, and emphasizing edges (Sekuler and Blake, 1994, pp. 76–78).

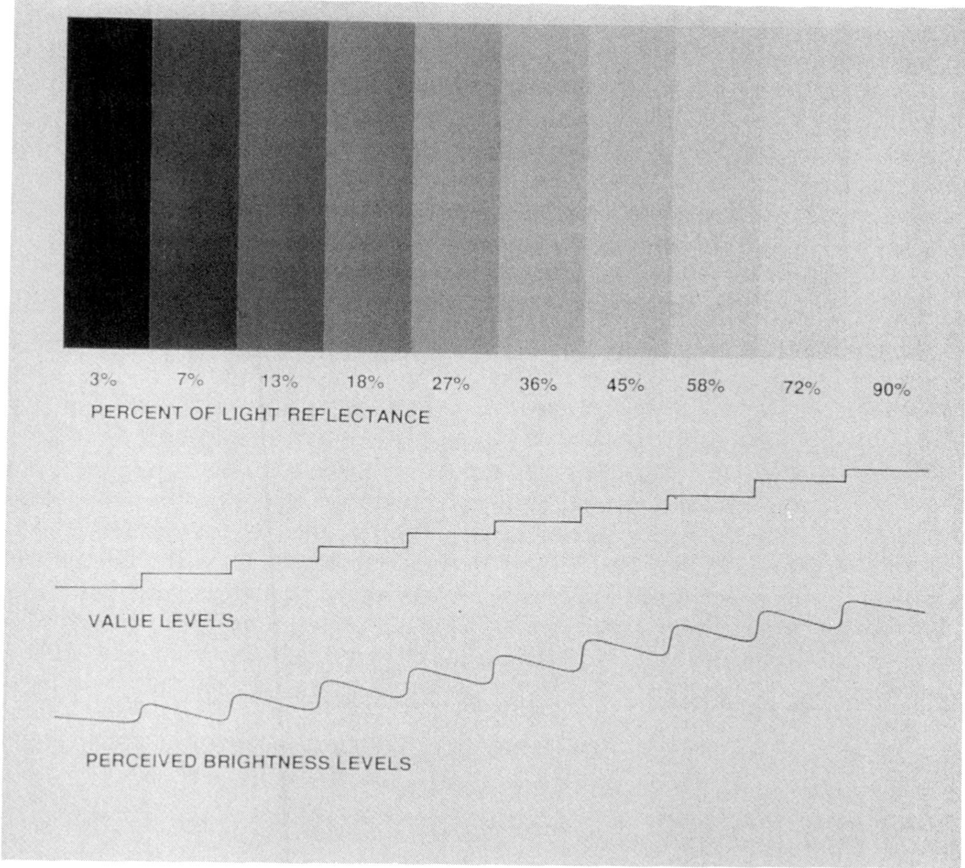

Measured and perceived brightness levels on a calibrated gray scale.

Although each stripe in a series is a flat, uniform color, it does not appear so. A rippling effect is observed as the colors in the series seem to "leapfrog" over one another, creating an effect known to designers as *fluting* and to scientists as *Mach bands* (Sekuler and Blake, 1994, p. 74). Any stripe series—whether of hues, values, or saturation levels, or combinations of two or all three of these—will flute if the color change is gradual and sequential. Mach bands are named for the man who first studied them seriously—the same man who may be better known to you for his work with the speed of sound.

COLOR EFFECTS DUE TO SIMULTANEOUS CONTRAST

A color can assume quite different guises as it interacts with other colors. Remember that appearance color is the "real" reality—what you see is what is!

Simultaneous contrast is intensified:

- where a large area of background color surrounds a small area of foreground color,
- where there is maximum edge contact between foreground and background colors, and
- where foreground shapes are small or open motifs rather than larger, denser shapes.

Intermixed colors are more susceptible to influence by other colors than are the more visually stable fundamental primary and secondary hues.

One Pigment Color Is Two or More Appearance Colors

A foreground color can be changed by the background color against which it appears.

Color Art 36 shows how a color can change one dimension at a time using simultaneous contrast. A background darker than the test color makes it appear lighter; a background lighter than the test color makes it appear darker (Color Art 36*A*). A background more saturated than the test color makes it appear less saturated; a background less sturated than the test color makes it appear more saturated (Color Art 36*B*). A background redder than the reddish-yellow test color makes it appear yellower; a background yellower than the test color makes it appear redder (Color Art 36C). Finally, backgrounds that differ maximally from each other are intended to create maximum differences in the test color (Color Art 36*D*).

5.2 FOREGROUND COLOR CHANGED BY BACKGROUND COLORS (Albers, 1963, p. 18)

Find two background colors that force out the greatest change in one foreground color. The background area must be considerably larger than the foreground in order to effect maximum change.

Did you change the hue, the value, or the saturation level of the foreground color? Or did you change two of these or all three? How can you change only one attribute of color at a time—its hue, its value, or its saturation—by controlling its background?

Two Pigment Colors Are One Appearance Color

Two colors can be changed by their backgrounds to appear as one color.

5.3 BACKGROUND COLOR MAKES TWO PIGMENT COLORS APPEAR AS ONE COLOR (Albers, 1963, p. 20)

a. Repeat the procedure in Exercise 5.2.

b. Substitute another color for one of the foreground colors so that both background colors appear the same.

Colors Are the Same as Their Reversed Grounds (Albers, 1963, p. 18)

Simultaneous contrast can make colors look like their reversed grounds (Color Art 37*A*). They also demonstrate how hue, value, and saturation can be controlled separately. Fluting scales may be useful in identifying colors for these exercises.

5.4 TWO FOREGROUND COLORS APPEAR TO BE THE SAME AS THEIR REVERSED GROUNDS (Albers, 1963, p. 18)

Find:

a. Three adjacent values from either a gray scale or a value scale of a hue.
b. Three adjacent hues of the same value and saturation level.
c. Three saturation levels of one hue.

Place a small amount of the center foreground color on larger backgrounds of the other two. What happens to the center color?

SIMULTANEOUS CONTRAST AT INTERIOR SCALE

Colors interact at environmental scale in the same way that they do in the cut paper exercises you do in the studio, except that areas are larger and colors are modified by the textures of materials and changing light conditions.

I remember a room whose cream colored walls were to be painted a very soft grayish blue. As the new color was being applied, it was transformed into a vicious, vivid blue that sent the owner into a state of panic. A test swatch of the blue appeared quite docile when viewed outside the room, so the decision was made to go ahead with it. Not until all of the cream color was covered, however, did the true receding quality of the blue become apparent.

Because of simultaneous contrast the blue was intensified by its juxtaposition with cream, a tint containing its orange complement. Had anyone noticed, the orange in the cream intermix was also being intensified by the blue, but at that time the concern was concentrated on the blue.

At interior scale there are many ways in which simultaneous contrast is a factor, such as where:

- a wall of one color is seen against a wall of another color,
- a painting is seen against a colored wall,
- differing floor and wall colors are juxtaposed,
- furniture of one color is seen against the floor or wall of another color,
- a curtain color is seen against a wall of another color, or
- an accessory is seen against another color background, such as a pillow on the sofa or a vase against a wall.

COMPLEMENTARY HUES AND THE EXTRA THIRD HUE

Some complementary hues are related to one another by a common third hue in the intermix of both (see Chapter 7). Under certain conditions the complementary interaction can be so strong that the subordinate hue is emanated as a third hue—a "ghost color":

- Bluish yellow (yellow-green) and bluish red (magenta) share blueness.
- Reddish yellow (yellow-orange) and reddish blue (reddish purple) share redness.
- Yellowish blue (cyan) and yellowish red (reddish orange) share yellowness.

The third color sometimes can be seen where complementary hues interact at a shared edge or where they are interspersed as dots on a white background. A red–green interaction is often involved, such as magenta and green or yellow green, in which the blueness common to both can be emanated as a third hue. This idea was suggested to me by Robert Irwin's dot paintings, in which a "mist" of color appeared to emanate from the surface of a painting. The effect here seems to be further strengthened by the interaction between yellowness and violet-blueness also present in the combination.

There are numerous variations of redness and greenness. Yellow-green with red-orange or yellow-green with yellow-orange can emit yellowness. In all of these combinations, you will find that whatever amount of complements are present in intermixtures, they will interact with each other. The common third hue appears as an elusive, possibly imagined wisp of hue emanated from the surface. Divisionist painting exploits this phenomenon.

Variously colored auras of subordinate hues can be emanated. Have you ever considered that tiny motifs of a reddish–greenish wallpaper could emit blueness or yellowness or grayness or lavenderness—depending on the common third hue present?

5.5 A "GHOST" COLOR EMANATED FROM COMPLEMENTARY HUES THAT SHARE A COMMON SUBORDINATE HUE

a. ***Interspersed small dots or thin lines of complementary or near complementary hues that share a common third hue.***

- *Bluish reds and bluish greens emit blueness.*
- *Yellowish reds and yellowish greens emit yellowness.*
- *Reddish yellows and reddish blues emit redness.*

The colors do not need to be highly saturated, the background should be white, and the viewing distance from several feet away.

How can you maximize the third or "ghost" color phenomenon? What particular values or saturation levels of the hues are most effective? How do viewing distance, size of color area, distances between colors, and illumination influence the effect?

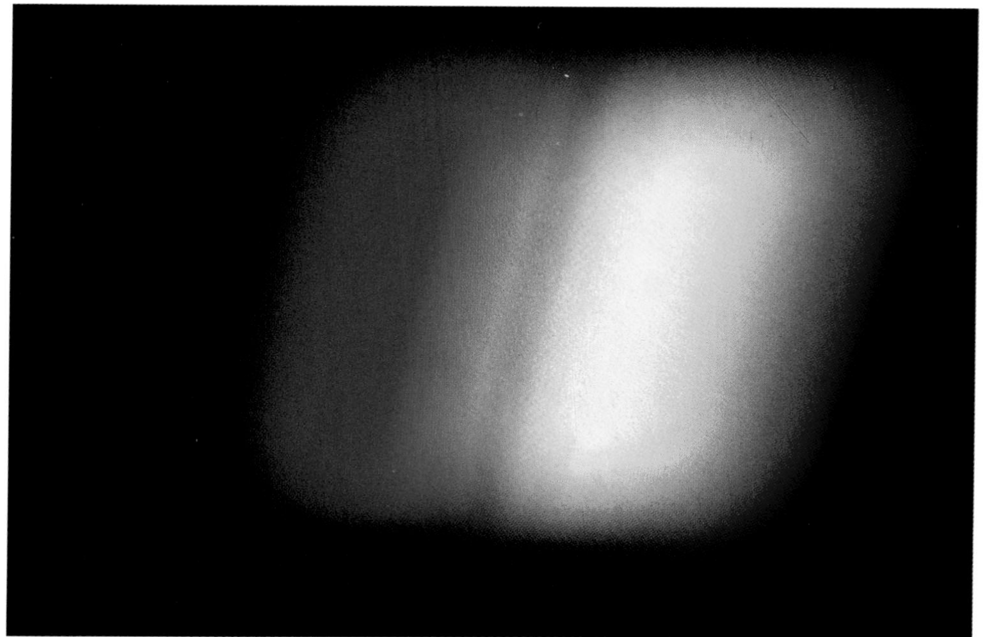

1 *Spectral hues become visible when light is directed through a prism.*

2 *The interior of a cube is redefined by surface color and design, creating an interior environment totally independent of the structure.*

COLOR AND THE ILLUSION OF VOLUMETRIC SPACE: COLOR CHAMBER

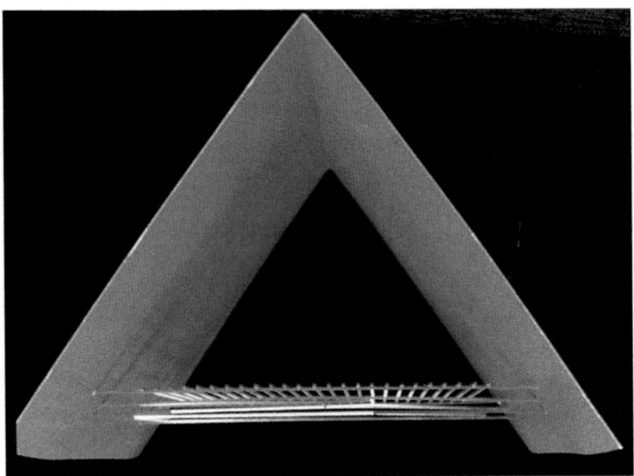

3A *Side view of color chamber showing linear elements grouped together at the widest part.*

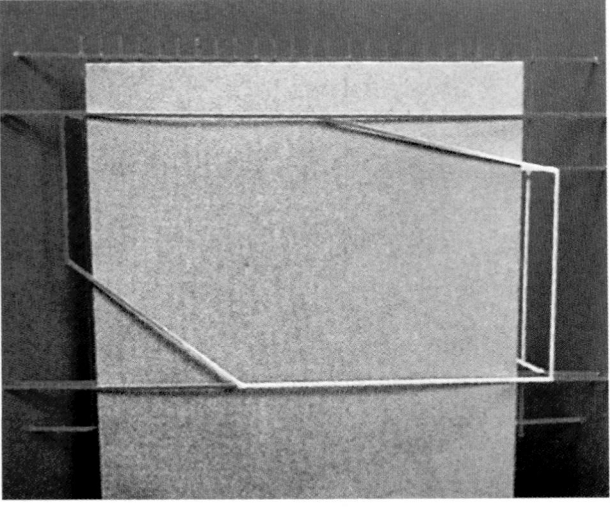

3B *Looking into the chamber, gray paper isolates the first layer of linear elements from those behind it.*

3C *Gray paper is moved behind the second layer of linear elements.*

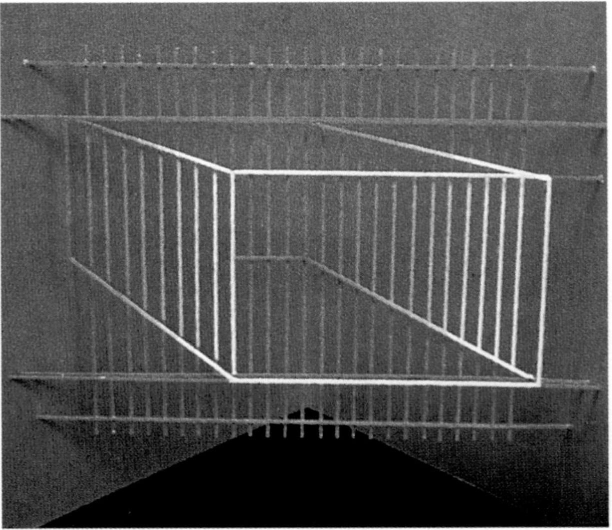

3D *Gray paper is removed to reveal the structure.*

4 *Dark ceiling creates interesting spatial effects.*

5 *This living room expresses energy and a strong personal statement.*

6 *Limited amounts of strong color define planes.*

7 *Detail is articulated by light, shade, and shadow in an all-white interior.*

8 *Color, pattern, and rich materials emphasize a corporate entryway.*

9 *Strong colors enhance an essentially white interior.*

11 *Adam Hall, Osterley Park, England. Circular configurations on floor and ceiling counter the rectangularity of the structure.*

10 *Field view of space shows elegant spacial relationships.*

12 *Mirrors double the space of a luxurious marble bathroom.*

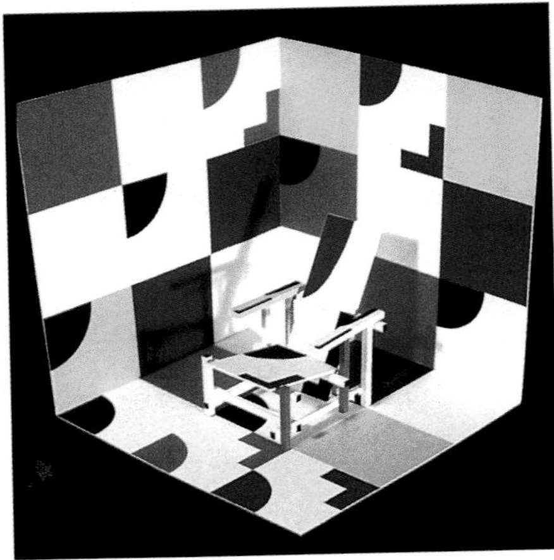

13 *Camouflage: Rietveld chair loses its identity in color and pattern.*

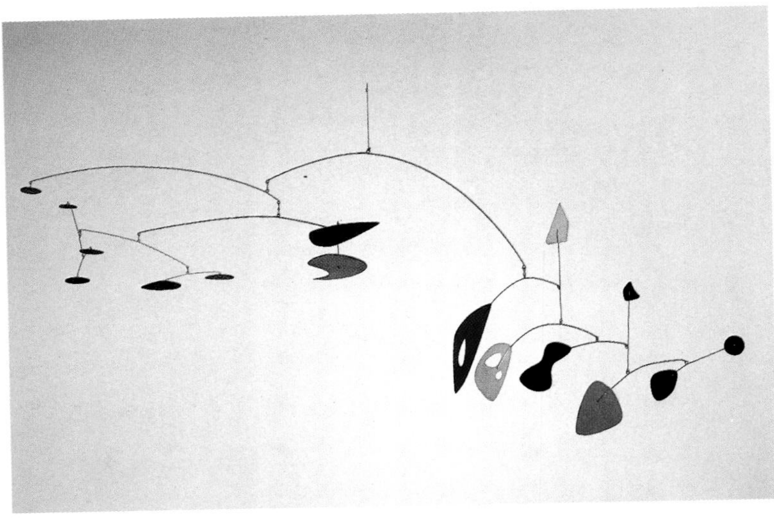

14 *"Yellow Sail" by Alexander Calder, 1950. Mobile defines the volume of space with wit, elegance, color, and movement.*

15 *Illusion of overlapping in a still-life painting. Light, shade, and shadow effects using the range of value and saturation levels between blue and yellow.*

16 *"The Yellow Wall" by Josef Albers. Illusion of solidity and transparency creates ambiguity.*

17 *"Bruges" by William Morris, 1811, reprinted 1925. Reversal of figure and ground.*

18 *Block-printed wallpaper, France, 1840–1860. Background–foreground relationships and the illusion of depth.*

19 *"April" by Jack Denst, 1963. Overlapping and the illusion of transparency.*

20 *"Mauer" by Le Corbusier, 1959. Two viewing distances: dots visible at close range but only the larger architectural scale configuration is seen from father away.*

21 *"Michaelmas Daisy" by J. H. Dearle, 1912. Unintended image.*

FIELD VIEW OF COLOR-SPACE FACADE: THE RELATIONSHIP BETWEEN LINE, FORM, VALUE, AND HUE

22A *A line drawing is made showing important shape elements of an entryway.*

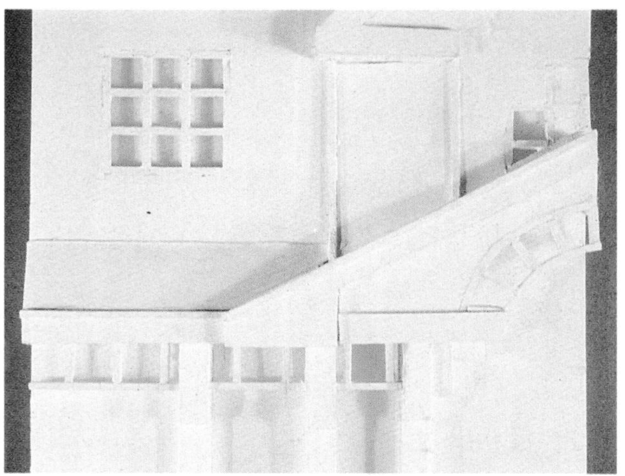

22B *From this a value drawing is made. On a scale of 1 to 10, lighter values are applied to shapes nearer the viewer and darker values to those farther away. A low-relief representation of the facade is made using a 1/6- or 1/4-inch foam core. The layers correspond to the value drawing, so that the nearest element is the lightest in value and the element farthest away is the darkest.*

22C *Colors of the student's own choosing enhance the sense of depth and indicate the change of materials.*

22D *Color is again used to minimize the visual/physical depth of the facade and alter the form as much as possible, so that it no longer looks like a place of entry but rather quite abstract.*

24A *When descending stairs only the treads are visible and steps may be difficult to see.*

23 *"Down the Stairs" by Joe Crivy. A man's field view as he descends the stairs, emphasizing the precariousness of the trip.*

24B *When ascending stairs both treads and risers are visible.*

25*A* *Surface texture gradient in paving stones.*

25*B* *"Multiple 1" by Robert Irwin, 1995. Structure both minimizes and maximizes convergence.*

25*C* *"Cathedral," origami greeting card design by Masahiro Chatani. Forced convergence.*

25*D* *Questionable convergence: lanterns.*

26 *As you move past columns, their relative positions change, enhancing the three-dimensional quality of the space. Movement is implicit in the background mural.*

27 *"Zigurat" by Robert Irwin, 1995. Space articulated by overlapping of transparent gauze.*

28 *Space is articulated by center sculpture and transparent materials.*

29A *Transition from dark to light value should exaggerate apparent depth, and from light to dark value should minimize apparent depth.*

29B *Transition from red to blue should exaggerate apparent depth, and from blue to red should minimize apparent depth.*

29C *Transition from yellow to blue should exaggerate apparent depth, and from blue to yellow should minimize apparent depth.*

30 *Blue House mural, In-Ouk Oh, architect. Vertical location of motifs creates the illusion of depth and distance, and the figures create the illusion of movement.*

31 *Iron grillwork: transparency, overlap, and movement.*

CORRIDOR CHALLENGES

Corridors are often unpleasant tube-shaped spaces. The design challenge is not only to solve the functional requirements but to make the space a pleasant place to be and the trip an interesting experience.

32B *Traditional Korean architecture. Here surfaces converge at a distant point, but posts and other architectural features create visual interest and enable the eye to gauge distances.*

32A *The passageway between Stouffer's Hotel, Nashville, and the mall is defined but not enclosed. Hangings, objects suspended in midair, tall plants, and architectural features provide color and relate the volume of space to human scale and make the trip a festive experience.*

32C *With no indicators with which to gauge depth and nothing to distract the eye, surfaces converge at a point on the distant horizon. The journey seems endless.*

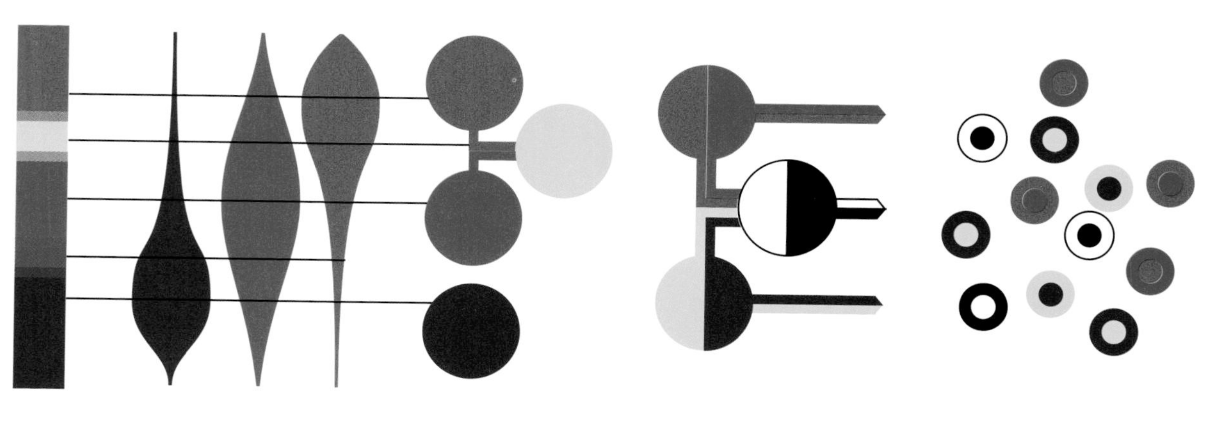

33A *Spectral hues in sunlight.*
33B *Cone response to light (Young–Helmholtz trichromatic theory).*
33C *Ganglion opponent process (Hering– Hurvitch–Jameson theory).*
33D *Brightness sensitivity is produced by combining red–green and yellow–blue signals.*
33E *The center–surround structure of the ganglions is responsive to edges.*

34A *Same hue and saturation, different values.*

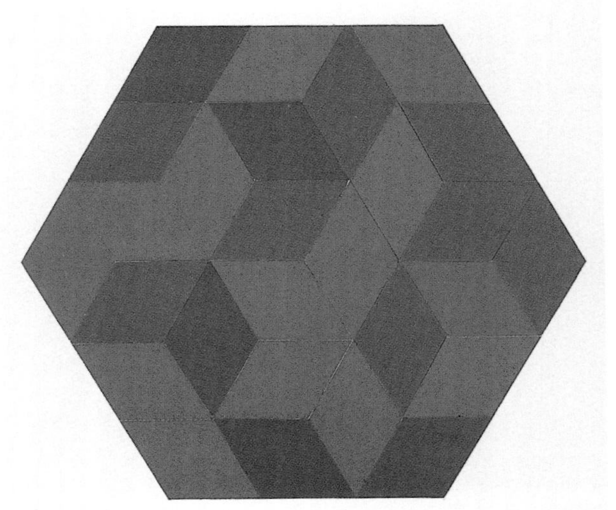

34B *Same hue and value, different saturation levels.*

34C *Same value and saturation, adjacent hues.*

34D *Same value and saturation, complementary or strongly contrasting hues.*

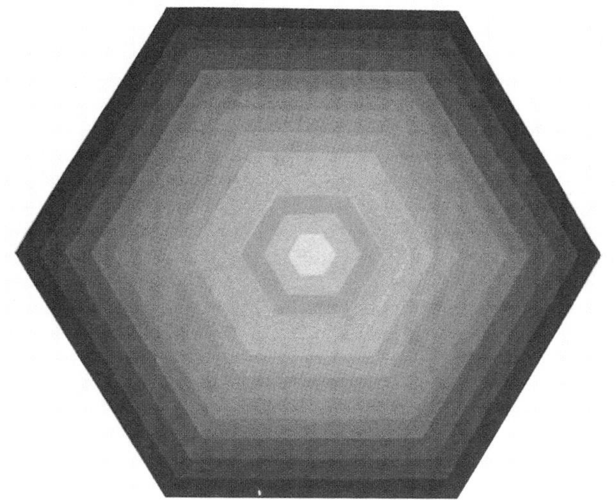

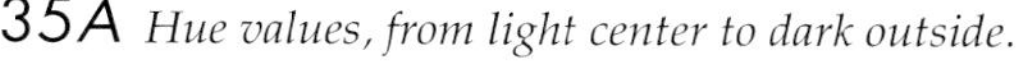

35*A* *Hue values, from light center to dark outside.*

35*B* *Hue values, from dark center to light outside.*

35*C* *Same or similar hue values.*

36A–D *Using simultaneous contrast to change a color one dimension at a time.*

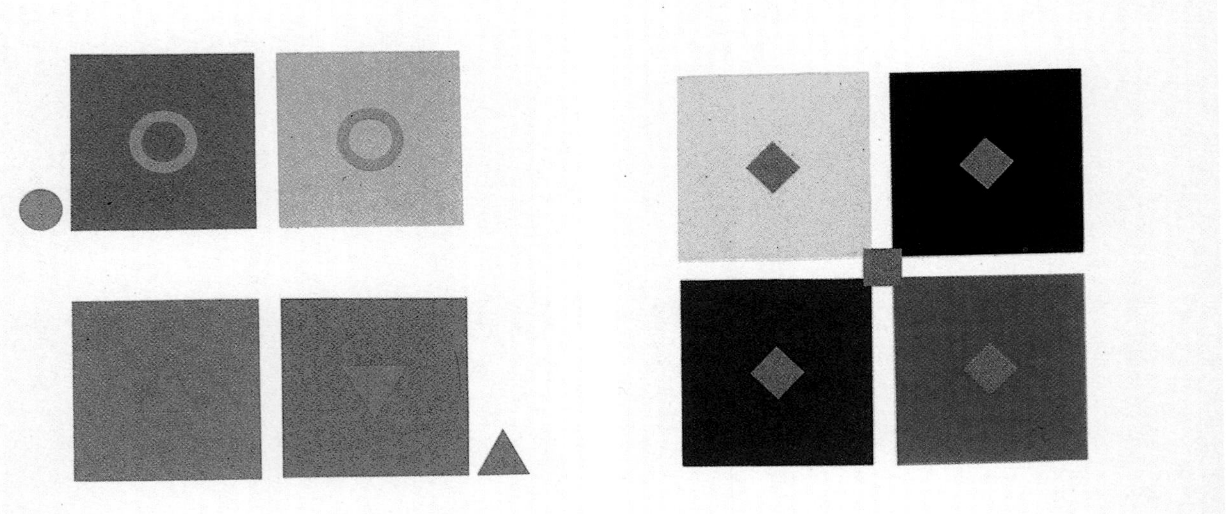

37A *One foreground color on two different backgrounds is made to resemble the opposite background. Each background color forces the foreground color in the direction of the other.*

37B *As you focus on the gray spot in the center, in your peripheral vision the gray spots on the four colored backgrounds assume the lively colors of their complements.*

38 *Divisionism, woven fabrics. At close range the weave is visible to both the form and color systems. (A) At a distance the colors merge. (B) Black darkens the colors instead of brightening them, as would be expected because of simultaneous contrast.*

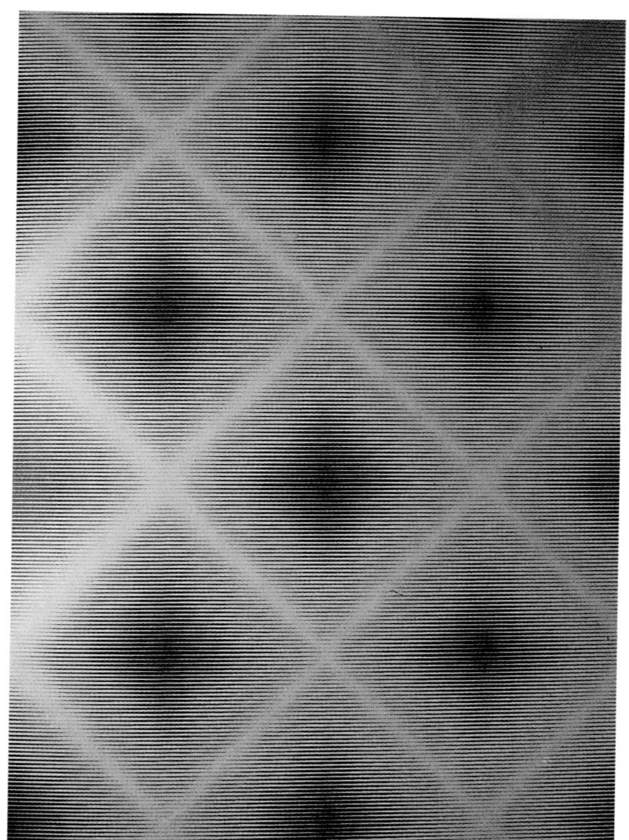

39 *"Whoops," from Bravo sample book, 1967–1968. Illusion of out-of-focus.*

40 *"Testura Grafica" by Gulio Alviani, 1971–1972. Illusion of movement.*

41A "Pink and Rose" wallpaper by William Morris, 1890, reprinted 1972. As yellow is darkened it becomes more dissonant with blue.

41B "Borage" wallpaper by William Morris, 1888–1889, reprinted 1972. Receding gray figure stands out in front of the red background.

41C "Samarkand," silk-screened velvet, by Jack Lenor Larsen. Each color appears as both background and foreground.

ARNHEIM'S SYNTAX OF HUES

The Arnheim system for analyzing the consonance and dissonance of hue combinations is based on the triangle of fundamental hues. The colors in the following examples are highly saturated and are useful primarily as a reference. Environment colors range over a wide spectrum of complex hue intermixtures, are almost always lower in saturation, and vary in value from tints through shades.

42A *The triangle of fundamental hues. Primaries ●, secondaries ■, and tertiaries or leading hues ➡.*

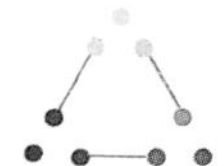

42B *Structural Inversion.*

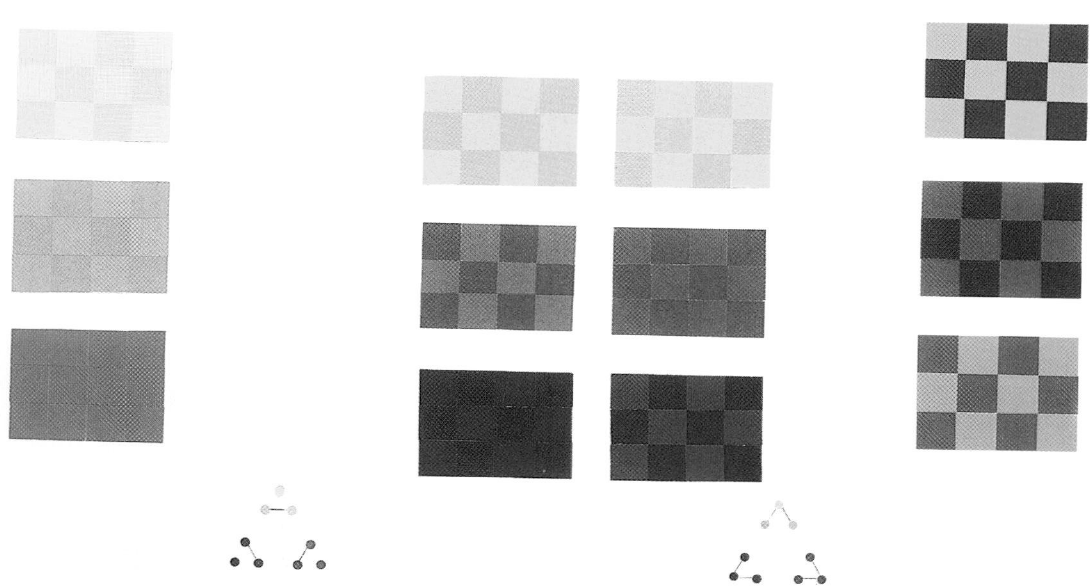

42C *Similarity of the Dominant.*

42D *A fundamental primary with a leading hue in which it is the dominant element.*

42E *Similarity of the Subordinate.*

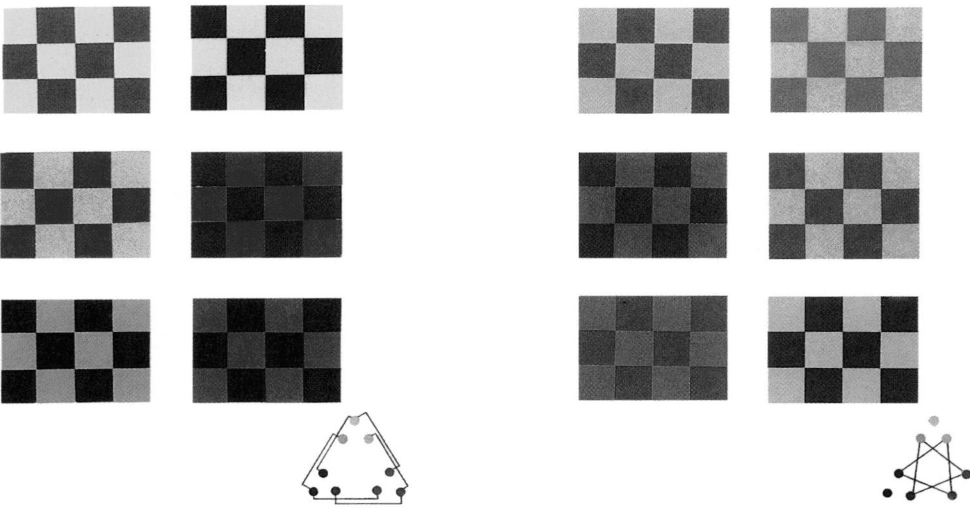

42F *Fundamental primary with a leading hue in which it is the subordinate element.*

42G *Structural contradiction for one common element.*

TRADITIONAL PRIMARY AND SECONDARY HUE RELATIONSHIPS

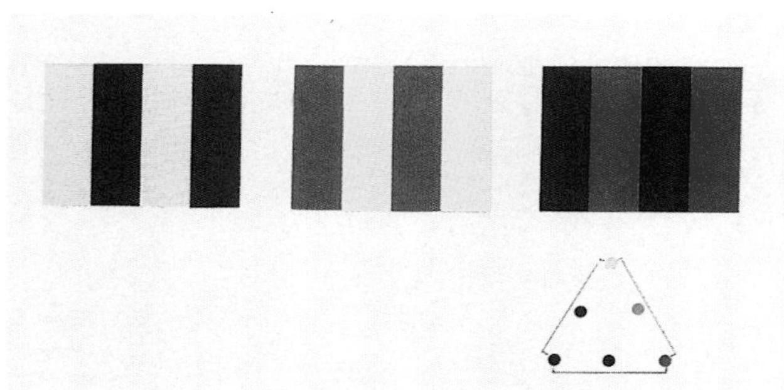

43A *Fundamental primary hue combinations.*

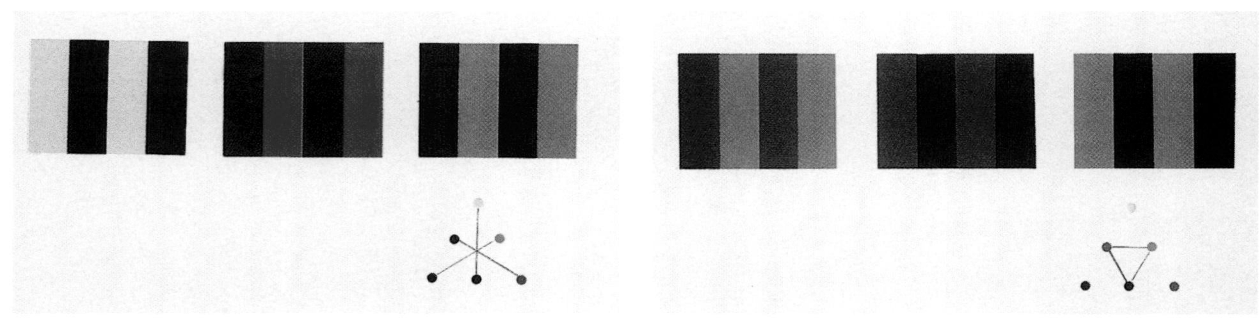

43B *Primary hue with its secondary complement.*

43C *Fundamental secondary hue combinations.*

44 *Warm and cool hue scales between yellow and violet in both (A) the natural order of values and (B) the reversed order of values. Note the fluting that occurs.*

45 *Complements: saturation scale between green and magenta.*

CAN YOU IDENTIFY THE TYPE OF HUE IN EACH OF THE FOLLOWING EXAMPLES?

46A *Natural order of values reversed (fundamental primary with a leading tone in which it is the dominant element).*

46B *Fundamental primary with a leading tone in which it is the subordinate element.*

46C *Natural order of values reversed (structural contradiction for one common element).*

46D *Structural inversion*

46E *Structural contradiction for one common element.*

46F *Fundamental primary with a leading tone in which it is the dominant element.*

46G *Structural inversion.*

46H *Similar value and saturation levels (similarity of the dominant).*

46I *Fundamental primary with a leading tone in which it is the subordinate element.*

46J *Low-saturation yellow+high-saturation purple (fundamental primary with its secondary complement).*

46K *Low values (fundamental primary with a leading hue in which it is the dominant element).*

46L *Fundamental primary with its secondary complement.*

46M *Same or similar values, high and low saturation, the natural order of values reversed (fundamental primary with leading tone in which it is the dominant element).*

46N *Low-saturation, low-value red+low-saturation yellow (fundamental primaries).*

46O *High values (structural contradiction for one common element).*

46P *Fundamental secondaries.*

46Q *Natural order of values reversed (structural inversion).*

46R *High-saturation blue+low-value, low-saturation orange (fundamental complements).*

46S *Similarity of the dominant.*

46T *Yellow tint + lower- value, lower-saturation yellow (monochromatic).*

46U *High saturation, same or similar values (similarity of the dominant).*

46V *Medium gray + low- saturation fundamental red (neutral + hue).*

46W *Structural contradiction for one common element.*

46X *Similarity of the dominant.*

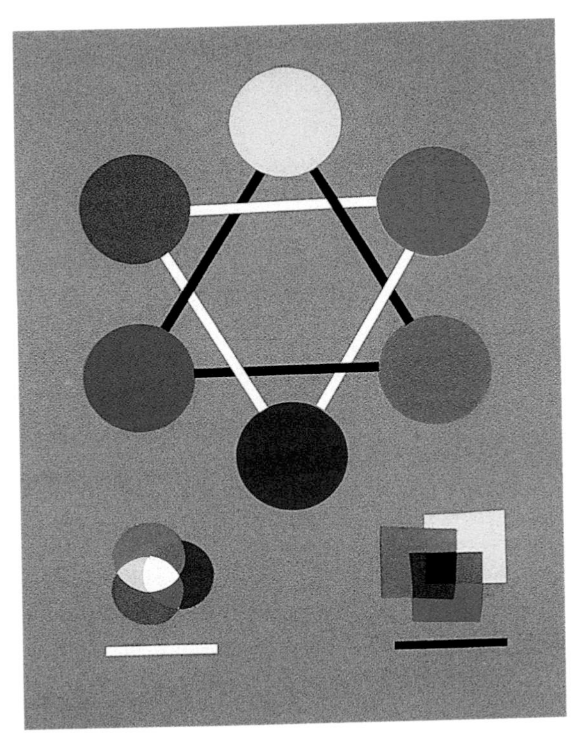

47 *Basic hues. Primary spectral hues are connected with a white line and primary pigment hues are connected with a black line. Spectral hues combine to create white light; pigment hues combine to create black.*

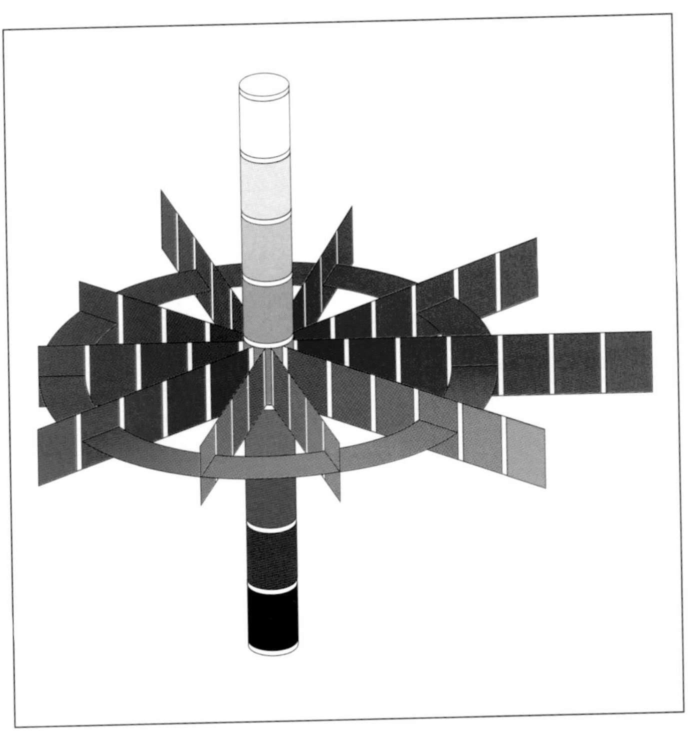

48 *Munsell color space showing value and saturation or chroma scales.*

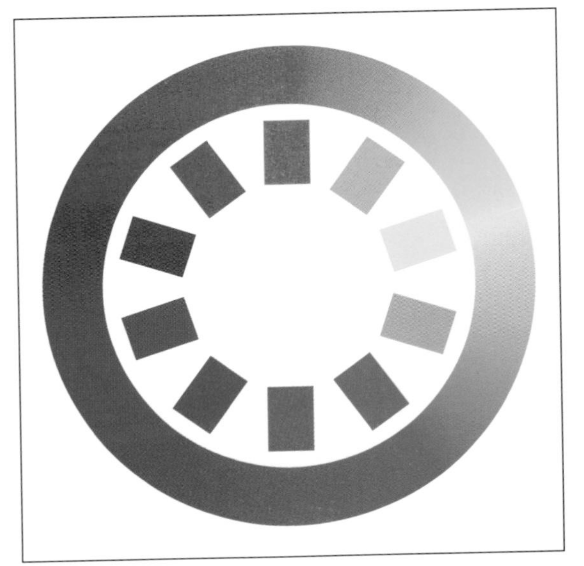

49 *Munsell hue circle.*

50 *Munsell color solid.*

51 *Earth colors produced by intermixing secondary hues—orange and green, orange and violet, and green and violet.*

52 *Sunny yellow background, soft wood tones, and sparse furnishings make a statement of elegant simplicity.*

53 *Dining room in Wellspring Retirement Community provides a warm, cheerful ambience.*

54 *Colors shown on sample board chosen to relate to colors of the natural world.*

55 *Otto Zenke showroom. Note the quiet dignity of subdued wood tones.*

EFFECTS OF VARIOUS TYPES OF ILLUMINATION ON HUES

Colors were photographed with tungsten-balanced film under the following light sources.

56A *Daylight.*

56B *Tungsten filament.*

56C *Tungsten halogen.*

56D *Fluorescent.*

56E *Combined daylight, incandescent, fluorescent, and halogen lights.*

57 *Embossed wallpaper, imitation leather, Japan, 1875-1899. Soft color imparts richness and warmth.*

58 *Shadow patterns cast by the plant create intricate patterns on the wall.*

59 *"Radial" by Robert Irwin, 1995. The space, itself, seems colored.*

60 *Lobby, First Union Bank, Greensboro, North Carolina. Reflections on the handsome, highly polished marble floor and walls along with the floor pattern and the contrast between patches of sunlight and shadow all serve to camouflage the structure and disrupt surface flatness. Especially on a sunny afternoon the floor could be confusing to the visually impaired.*

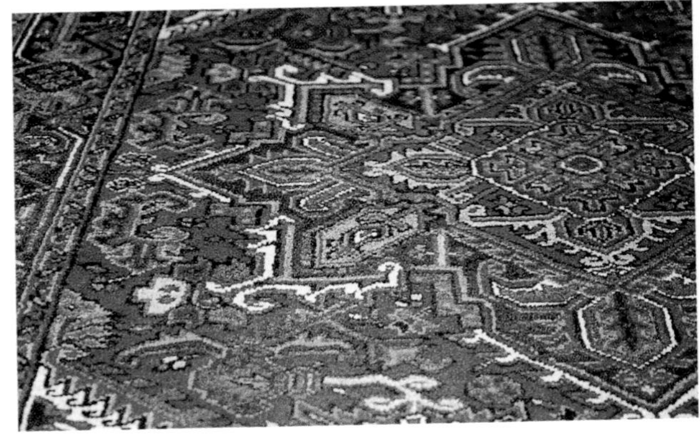

61 *Colors appear richer and deeper when looking into the directional pile of the rug rather than when looking across it.*

Two complementary colors force out a shared subordinate hue along a contact edge as a "ghost color." *This may be difficult to achieve, and you may have to experiment with several pairs to find two that work. The subordinate hue repeated nearby or somewhere in the design may help to emphasize the effect.*

OPTICAL COLOR MIXING

Optical mixing is the opposite of simultaneous contrast, which accentuates color differences. Optical mixing annuls differences.

Color photographs in newspapers are composed of tiny dots of yellow, cyan, and magenta in various combinations. The colors are printed separately but are mixed by the eye to create the desired image. The range of grays in black-and-white images is created by visual mixtures of tiny black dots of various sizes with the white of the background paper. Because the individual dots are too small to be discriminated by either the color system or the form system, they bleed or blend as the colors are mixed optically.

In pointillist paintings, sometimes called divisionist or partitive paintings, colors are optical mixtures, and often larger dots or brush marks are used. In such paintings and in some tweed fabrics and mosaics, the individual dots or spots are large enough to be distinguished at close range by the form system, yet bleed when viewed from a few feet away. When dots can be seen by both the form system and the color system, they no longer bleed (Livingstone, 1988, pp. 84–85). Viewing distance may be the determining factor.

Consider, for example, the woven fabrics shown in Color Art 38. At close range details of the weave are visible to both the color and the form systems, but at a distance the colors are mixed by the eye as in a pointillist or divisionist painting. This is the opposite of simultaneous contrast. Where black threads are woven into the fabric, they darken the colors rather than making them appear brighter or lighter (Color Art 38*A*). Where threads of different hues are woven together, the colors intermix when seen at a distance (Color Art 38*B*).

When seen from close range, as when looking at a wallpaper book, a design may appear as small individual red and blue dots or motifs on a white or off-white background, but when viewed from across a room, the red and blue dots could merge into purple or possibly emanate purple as a third hue. If the dominant colors in the room are pure red and pure blue, purple could be a clashing intruder.

A cleverly contrived design could be interesting from both near and far viewing distances, seen perhaps as small interesting dot figures at close range but as a larger unit, such as a mural or landscape painting, when viewed from across the room. The wallpaper design by Le Corbusier (Color Art 20) is seen as small dots at close range, but they merge when seen from across the room. The design is unique in its architectural scale and the different configurations possible, depending on how it is installed.

5.6 COLOR BLEEDING VERSUS COLOR CONTRAST

Create a design that is interesting at two viewing distances. Use dots or other small motifs that would be suitable as an interior wallcovering. From across the room the dots should merge to create a composite, larger-scale design. Where would such a design be suitable?

SUCCESSIVE CONTRAST

THE AFTERIMAGE

If you stare fixedly at a color image, the ganglions become saturated and the image becomes temporarily engraved on the retina. If the glance is diverted to a white surface, the image follows your glance and a negative afterimage appears in the color of the complement. As the positive ganglion channel switches off, the opposite channel is activated: ON yellow, therefore, becomes OFF yellow, and blue takes over the afterimage. This is regarded as evidence of the *theory of ganglion opponency* (Sekuler and Blake, 1994, p. 202). Afterimages can also be considered a kind of "ghost color."

The afterimage provides a way of determining the exact complement of a hue. It was once supposed that red and green were complementary hues, but red or orange-red evokes a cyan afterimage and green evokes magenta. Blue and yellow intermixes were once thought to produce green, but a vivid green was not forthcoming. Violet-blue evokes a yellow afterimage and vice versa, with green nowhere in the formula. If you stare at a black-and-white image on the television screen, the afterimage will be white and black.

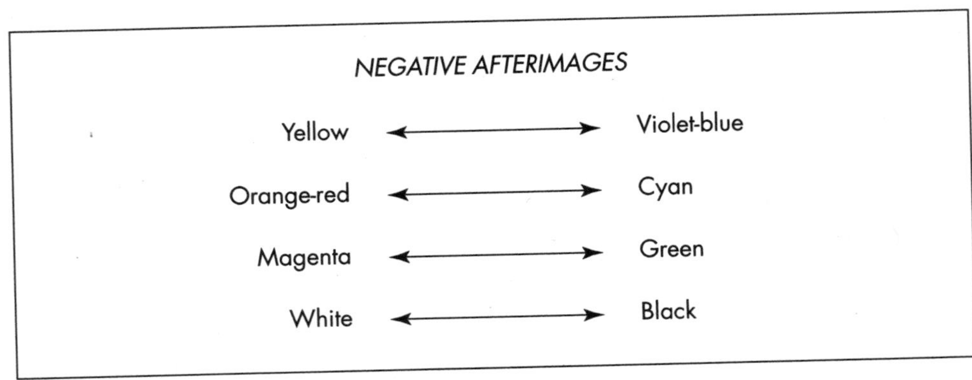

If the glance is diverted to a colored background, the afterimage is seen as a mixture of its complement and the background hue. For example, if your retina is saturated with an orange-red image and your glance falls on a yellow background, your cyan afterimage blends with yellow to become a yellow-green afterimage, making the yellow background appear even yellower.

If the glance is diverted to the same color as the afterimage, the eye is deprived of its proper afterimage and the result is visual instability.

GRAY THAT ISN'T GRAY

The successive contrast is apparent in other ways. For instance, a gray swatch on a magenta background appears to be tinged with green, whereas the same gray swatch on a green background has a magenta cast (Color Art 37*A*). When yellow and red–orange threads were woven into a gray fabric, the illusion of blues and cyans appeared (Chevreul in Sekuler and Blake, 1985, p. 202). These, too, are "ghost" colors.

Because of ganglion opponency a color seeks its complement and, if it is not present, the ganglions invent it. The eye saturated with green sees magenta on a neutral gray (Color Art 37*B*); as the ganglions become fatigued, green is switched OFF and magenta is switched ON.

SUCCESSIVE CONTRAST AT INTERIOR SCALE

Moving from a green interior into a gray room should elicit the same response as that cited previously. The brightness and hue of a room you enter will be influenced by the brightness and hue of the room you just left. To an eye adapted to darkness, a bright room will appear even brighter. "A magenta will appear more intense if we have seen a cyan first. A yellow will look yellower if the eye is adapted to a blue surface just before viewing, etc." (Gerritsen, 1983, p. 138).

Color areas viewed sequentially within a room or in a surface pattern will also be affected by successive contrast.

5.7 SUCCESSIVE CONTRAST

Place small gray foreground motifs on two or more background hues. Make comparisons and choose a pair in which maximum hue differences between the two grays are apparent. How large must a background area be in relation to the gray motifs in order to evoke a successive contrast response? What are optimal sizes and shapes for the gray motifs?

OPTICAL ART AND WALLPAPER

The optical or retinal art movement of the 1960s and 70s broke with earlier tradition in that the focus of a painting moved from the outside world to the painting as an optical experience and to entering "the incompletely explored region area between the cornea and the brain" (Seitz, 1965, p. 9). Color elements were given maximum freedom of operation in every direction (Seitz, 1965, p. 12)

Despite artists' protestations about the serious intent of their creations, much of the optical or retinal art that became popular during the 1960s and 1970s has a decorative quality that seems ready-made for wallpaper.

In optical art visual challenges are rampant—mazes, figures that reverse themselves, unstable boundaries between colors, implied movement on a flat surface (Color Art 39 and 40), and so on. Some black-and-white designs appear to have color, and others employ afterimage and border-contrast effects (Bloomer, 1976, p. 30). Fluting, simultaneous and successive contrast, the bleaching of color-sensitive cones, the aggressive confrontations of hues, units that pulsate, and pointillism that neutralizes opposites rather than intensifying them—all of these phenomena and others were employed (Seitz, 1965, p. 18).

Shimmering or vibrating effects can be experienced when looking at designs composed of closely spaced lines. This results from the constant rapid oscillations of the eye that are a part of normal vision. The bizzare effects of shimmering black and white striped wallpaper, however, would not be recommended for homes or places of work (Bloomer, 1976, p. 30), although complex patterns based on such optical effects can be developed for surface enrichment.

How important or aggressive or challenging should an interior background surface be? At what point does wallpaper assume the importance of a painting or a mural? Could optical phenomena be desirable as a compelling way to attract attention or enliven an area? If a design "hurts your eyes" or engenders nausea or dizziness or "drives you crazy" trying to figure it out, it would not be desirable for an interior environment. However, if its purpose is to attract momentary attention, to amuse, to intrigue—why not?

HARMONIC RELATIONSHIPS OF HUES

Color is the music of design, but "so long as we hear only single notes, we do not hear music" (Albers, 1963, p. 5). At no time is the parallel between color and music more apparent than when considering harmonic relationships. "Good" interior color depends not only on individual color quality but also on how colors relate to one another harmonically. Optical interactions are natural phenomena, but harmonic interactions require an æsthetic judgment.

As we examine the harmonic quality of various hue combinations, we shall see how they may be affected by their values and saturation levels.

TRADITIONAL COLOR SCHEMES

COLOR CIRCLE GEOMETRY

Traditional color schemes are based on the geometry of the fundamental hue circle. Fundamental hues include the visually "pure," single-ingredient primaries—red, yellow, and blue (○) and the visually balanced "pure" secondaries—green, orange, and purple (□).

Yellow
○
Green □ □ Orange
Blue ○ ○ Red
□
Purple

FORMULA COLOR SCHEMES

- *Monochromatic color schemes* are drawn from shades, tints, and tones of one hue or a neutral. They are the safest, most conservative of color combinations, and are widely used as backgrounds in interiors.
- *Complementary color schemes* are based on colors diametrically opposite one another on a hue circle. When skillfully fine-tuned they can be quite agreeable, and because of ganglion opponency and the negative afterimage, it has been postulated that they not only require one another but provide satisfying aesthetic balance. Some artists avoid them, however, because the way they intensify one another can create jarring discord.
- *Split complementary color schemes* share characteristics of complementary hues, but the addition of a hue immediately adjacent to one or both of the complementary pairs increases the complexity of the combination.
- *Contrasting color schemes* are combinations of either two or three hues taken from any triad relationship on the color circle. They can be either harmonious or clashing, depending on the composition of the individual hues and how they are used.
- *Adjacent color schemes* are taken from a small arc on the hue circle. They are inherently complex relationships—some combinations clashing, others blending smoothly.

FORMULA COLOR SCHEMES CHALLENGED

Formula color schemes tell you what colors are "supposed to go together," and for a very long time the formulas were believed to ensure harmonious color combinations.

Critics point out that formula color schemes have been employed as a crutch for the timid and insecure in their search for safe, nice, pretty colors that are calculated to offend no one. Whether any color combination, formula or otherwise, works well or poorly for interior or any other use depends on the *artistry of the designer* rather than on the formulas themselves.

Arnheim expresses fundamental objections to the principle on which agreeable color harmonies are based and to the rules of color harmony presumed to create them:

> *The principle conceives of a color composition in which everything fits everything. All local relations between neighbors show the same pleasant conformity. Obviously this is the most primitive kind of harmony, suitable at best for the so-called color schemes of clothing or rooms, although there seems to be no reason why even a dress or a bedroom should cling to a noncommittal homogeneity of color rather than setting accents, creating centers of attention, separating elements by contrast. Certainly a work of art based on such a principle could describe nothing but a world of absolute peace, devoid of action, expressing only a static over-all mood. It would represent that state of deadly serenity at which, to use the language of the physicist, entropy approaches a maximum.* (Arnheim, 1954, p. 285)

Albers states:

...we may forget for a while those rules of thumb of complementaries, whether complete or "split," and of triads and tetrads as well. They are worn out. (Albers, 1963, p. 42)

...no mechanical color system is flexible enough to precalculate the manifold changing factors...in a single prescribed recipe.... (Albers, 1963, p. 42)

We emphasize that color harmonies, usually the special interest or aim of color systems, are not the only desirable relationships. As with tones in music, so with color—dissonance is as desirable as its opposite, consonance. (Albers, 1963, p. 68)

The rules became obsolete by the 1950s and 60s, influenced by the heyday of optical art and the psychedelic experience, by Alexander Girard and his uninhibited use of vivid Mexican color, by Charles Eames with his exuberant use of color in daily life, by Mary Quant and miniskirts in shocking dissonances, and by many others. Exuberance in color, often expressing a sense of rebelliousness, fit the public mood of the day. Formulas are not now and never have been foolproof recipes for agreeable color combinations. *There are, in fact, no foolproof formulas for "good" color combinations.*

HUE RELATIONSHIPS

HARMONY DEFINED

The dictionary definition of harmony is "fitting together" or "agreement" (Webster). This is what Arnheim had in mind when he said that "harmony is essential in the sense that all the colors of a composition must fit together in a unified whole if they are to be reliable" (Arnheim, 1954 p. 284). Although he was referring to color in paintings, the same principle holds for color at interior scale.

For centuries the rules of harmony have been the basis for Western music, but 19th- and 20th-century composers increasingly have abandoned traditional harmonic restrictions in the search for new modes of expression. A parallel can be drawn with changing color uses over time, as the desire for agreeable color in fashion and design is frequently superseded by the restless search for new and unusual color experiences more expressive of prevailing currents of thought and feeling. Conflict and upheaval in modern society are reflected in the dissonances and discords of both the music and the colors that surround us today.

There are no new spectral or basic hues to be discovered, but there are infinite ways of intermixing them to create "new" colors, and there are infinite ways of combining colors to produce "new" harmonic relationships.

CONSONANCE, DISSONANCE, AND DISCORD

Where two or more hues appear together, a harmonic relationship exists. This relationship can be consonant, dissonant, or discordant.

- *Consonance* implies concord or agreeable colors, colors that attract or enhance one another, colors that blend or "go together."
- *Dissonance* implies sour notes, unexpected, often jarring colors that "wake you up," that inject an element of surprise, or that provide relief from cloying prettiness, blandness, or sweetness.
- *Discord* implies disagreeable conflict, harsh, grating color combinations that "set your teeth on edge."

Envision a continuum with consonance at one extreme, discord at the other, and dissonance somewhere in between. Lines that separate consonance, dissonance, and discord cannot be drawn with confidence, because these are judgments that involve people's feelings about them, and there can exist wide differences in their opinions.

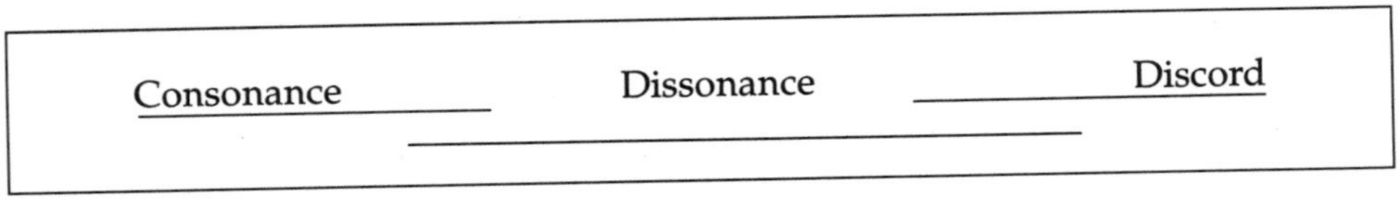

Consonance	Dissonance	Discord

One person may like only pretty, consonant color combinations, whereas another may find the same colors bland and boring. One person may find dissonant colors daring and exciting, whereas another may find them disturbing. One person's favorite color combination could be regarded by another as discordant, beauty being in the eye of the beholder. The response to color combinations is highly subjective and influenced by the cultural setting.

We do not usually seek discord for the interiors we inhabit, but it can be useful for expressing how we feel about what we do not like. Legend has it that in the Madison White House a drawing room was painted a bilious green on the presumption that the ladies would consider it unflattering and retire elsewhere after dinner, leaving the gentlemen to enjoy their cigars in their own company. It is also rumored that Mme. DuBarry found out what her rival would be wearing and had the ballroom decorated in a color that would clash with the rival's dress.

Our interest here is focused on consonance and dissonance in hue relationships. At the close of the 20th century, we often find dissonant color combinations to be more beautiful and intriguing than more consonant combinations and often more expressive of the mood and temper of the day.

What follows is Arnheim's system for objectively defining consonance and dissonance.

HUE PAIR RELATIONSHIPS

Pair relationships are the building blocks from which color combinations are constructed. The more hues appearing together in a design, the greater the number of pair relationships.

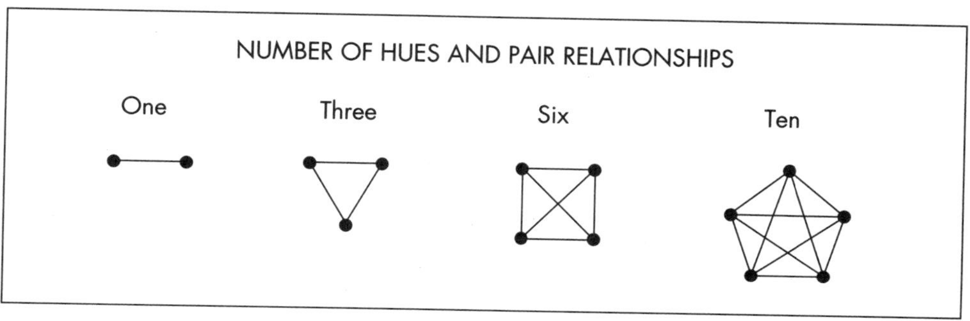

Color Art 41*A* is a two-hue combination with one interaction, and Color Art 41*B* is a three-hue combination with three interactions. The more colors in a pattern or an interior, the greater the number of interactions.

The Jack Lenore Larsen silk-screened velvet, "Samarkand," shown in Color Art 41*C* shows 10 process colors printed on the selvedge. Ten process colors generate 45 separate interactions, but this is only the beginning. There are a number of simultaneous contrast interactions, and divisionist techniques create still more colors as small dots and stripes of one color are printed on another color background. Transparent dyes are applied in successive layers, creating new colors where they overlap. Aside from its artistic merit, the sheer complexity of such a design can rivet the attention and maintain interest for a considerable period of time, as does a painting.

Designer's Guide to Color, Volumes 1 and 2, catalogues thousands of two-hue and hundreds of three-hue combinations at various values and saturation levels. These are oriented toward graphics design for the publishing industry but have implications for interior and pattern uses. *Designer's Guide to Color,* Volume 3, illustrates the effects of pattern on color relationships and is oriented toward textile design and the fashion industry.

ARNHEIM'S SYNTAX OF MIXTURES

THE TRIANGLE OF FUNDAMENTAL HUES

"The sensations of black, white, yellow, blue, and red are fundamental in the sense of being irreducible perceptually" (Arnheim, 1954, p. 288). These colors are the primaries in the fundamental hue system, and green, orange, and purple are the secondaries.

In Arnheim's system for categorizing hue relationships, fundamental hues are shown in a triangle in which the primaries—pure red, pure yellow, and pure blue—are positioned at the points:

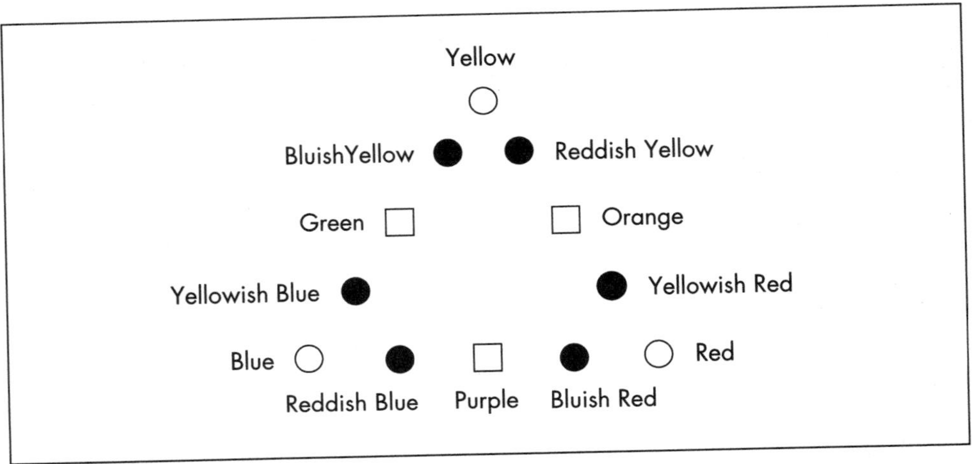

Secondaries and tertiaries or leading hues are positioned on the scales between the primaries (Color Art 42*A*). The three scales are:

- Red to blue
- Blue to yellow
- Yellow to red

The triangle is a structure that makes it possible to assess the symmetry or asymmetry of hue relationships:

- Symmetrical relationships are generally consonant.
- Asymmetrical relationships are generally dissonant.

Types of Hues

Primaries are maximally different from each other, and are the most stable and self-contained of all colors. In combinations with intermixed hues, they stand out as unrelated hues, "sticking out" like the proverbial "sore thumb." In other words, they are destined to be dissonant or discordant elements in combinations with more complex hues.

Each of the fundamental secondaries (□), green, orange, and purple, is a visually balanced intermixture of two parent primaries. Like primaries, the secondaries are highly stable and unrelatable and are, therefore, dissonant or discordant in combinations with the more complex tertiaries.

Leading or tertiary hues lie between primary and secondary hues on the scale between any two primaries. (Arnheim uses the term "leading tones" rather than "leading hues," but in this book "tone" is used to designate degree of saturation.) One parent primary is the dominant ingredient in a tertiary intermix, and the other parent primary is the subordinate ingredient. Tertiaries appear as "deviations from a dominant fundamental" and are seen as pressing toward it (Arnheim, 1954, p. 290). Because they are unbalanced, tertiaries are "highly dynamic, and prone to interact with other colors and, for this reason, particularly inviting for pictorial composition" (Arnheim in Garau, 1993, p. xi).

When identifying a leading hue, the dominant element is expressed as a noun and the subordinate element as an adjective. Magenta is described as bluish red, and green as bluish yellow or yellowish blue, depending on which primary is dominant in the intermix. Chartreuse is bluish yellow, and cyan is yellowish blue.

As noted previously, the fundamental hues differ from the basic hues in that all of the basic hues except yellow are leading hues. Most of the colors in the environment, indoors or outdoors, are leading hues, most are complex intermixtures, and few, if any, are of maximum saturation.

Consonance and Dissonance

Arnheim identifies six hue relationships (Arnheim, 1954, pp. 290–293) that include different types of adjacent, complementary, and contrasting colors. Some of these are considered consonant and others, dissonant.

Consonant hue combinations appear to combine easily with one another, to "go together," to be mutually attracting. When juxtaposed they can fuse or blend. When values are held constant, the edge between them is less distinct than the edge between colors that clash.

Dissonant hue combinations are separated by clash or mutual repulsion.

When testing Arnheim's syntax of mixtures, it is important to use leading hues in which there is definite dominance of a primary in the intermix unless a polar primary is indicated.

Wucius Wong's *Principles of Color Design* (Wong, 1987, pp. 63–97) illustrates with ingenious designs many of the harmonic relationships discussed here.

Augusto Garau's *Color Harmonies* illustrates the Arnheim syntax of mixtures (Garau, 1993, plates 1–40) and discusses the following color relationships.

ADJACENT HUE RELATIONSHIPS

Structural Inversion

Here two hues lie on the same scale of the triangle between two fundamental hues. They share the same two primary ingredients, but in differing proportions (Color Art 42*B*):

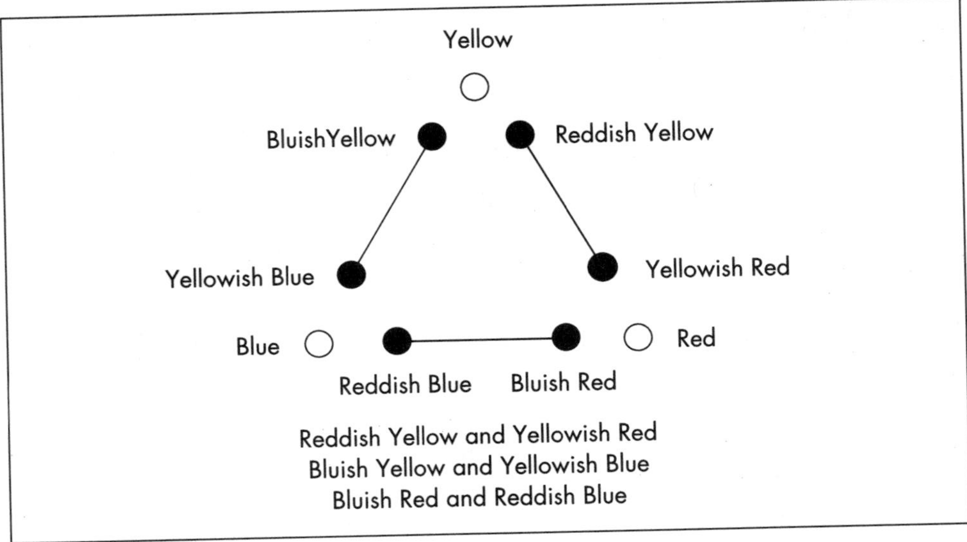

In this kind of symmetrical relationship, the colors are generally experienced as blending or consonant. If values are held constant or nearly so, the edges between them appear to be nonexistent. As the two hues lie farther apart on the scale, they may be considered more contrasting than adjacent.

Similarity of the Dominant

Here adjacent hues lie on either side of a primary. In both of these hues, one primary is the dominant element but the subordinate element in each is different (Color Art 42C):

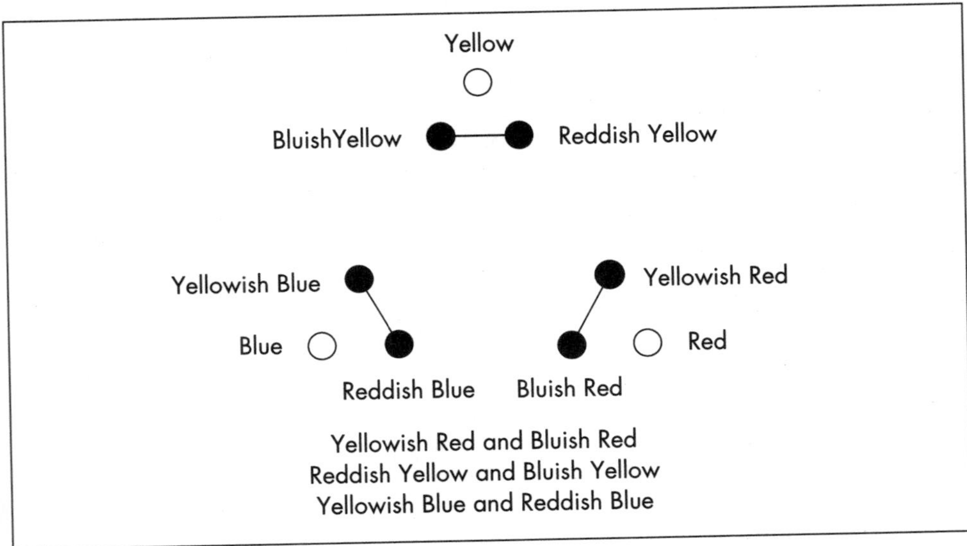

The dominant hue is torn in two different directions as the subordinate is drawn from two scales. Although the effect seems to be jarring, this is a popular use of dissonance. If values are held constant, edges between two hues from this group are more pronounced than in structural inversion. Bluish yellow and reddish yellow—chartreuse and orange-yellow—are the logo colors for a pickle company.

A Fundamental Primary with a Leading Hue in Which It Is the Dominant Element

Here the adjacent hues consist of a primary and a hue in which that same primary is the dominant element (Color Art 42*D*):

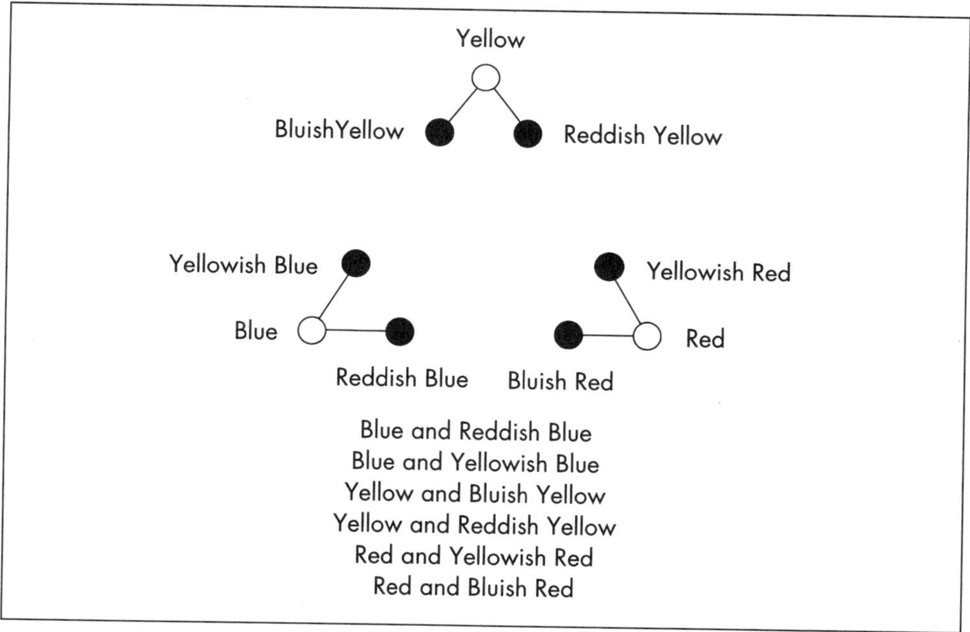

The pure primary and the intermix are asymmetrical, and because a visually pure primary is essentially unrelatable to a leading hue, these hues clash more strongly than do hues in structural inversion. If values are held constant, edges tend to be distinct.

COMPLEMENTARY HUE RELATIONSHIPS

Similarity of the Subordinate

Because hues in this relationship lie opposite one another on the hue triangle and diametrically opposite one another on the hue circle, they are, therefore, complementary. They differ from primary–secondary complementaries in that they share a third hue as the subordinate element (Color Art 42*E*):

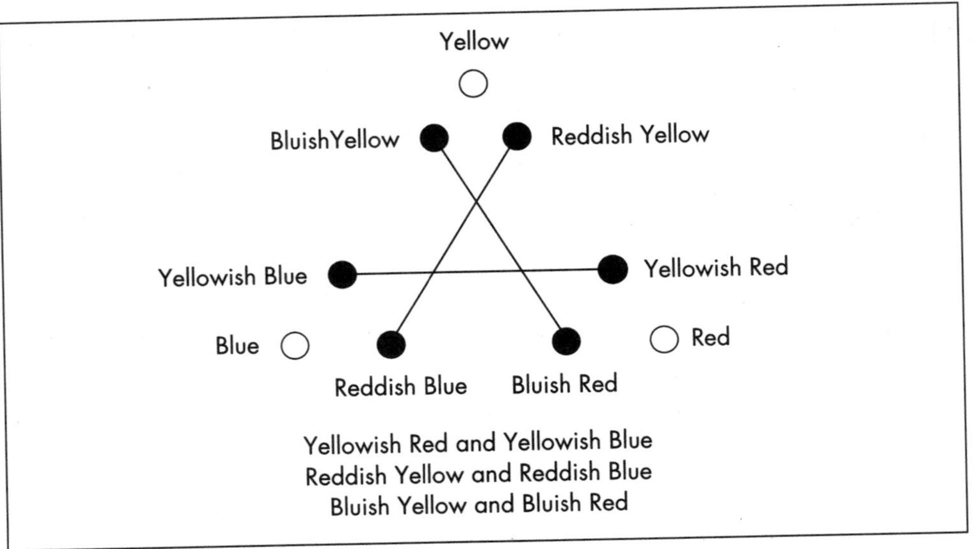

Here the "structural similarity makes for a ready attraction" or consonance (Arnheim, 1954, p. 291). The shared subordinate hue serves as a common denominator or transitional element, making this combination more harmonious than a primary–secondary complementary relationship in which there is no common element.

CONTRASTING HUE RELATIONSHIPS

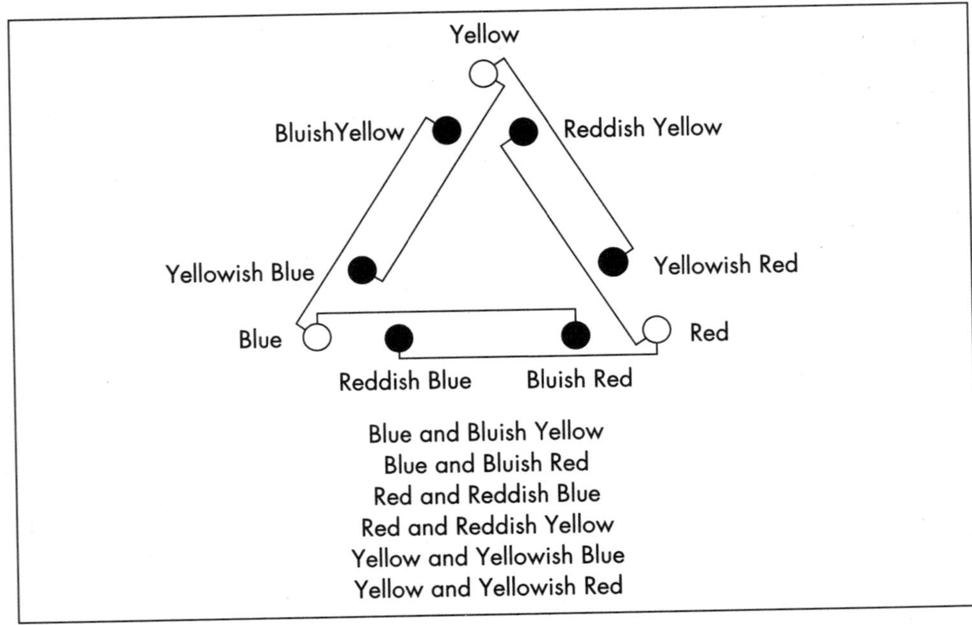

A Fundamental Primary with a Leading Hue in Which It Is the Subordinate Element

In this relationship (p. 80) a polar primary hue is paired with a hue mixture in which that same primary is the subordinate element (Color Art 42*F*):

The primary also appears as the subordinate element in the intermix, the asymmetry of which is cause for conflict. This combination seems to be even more discordant than the combination of a polar primary with a leading hue in which it is the dominant element.

Structural Contradiction for One Common Element

A primary hue is the dominant element in one intermixture and the subordinate element in the other (Color Art 42*G*):

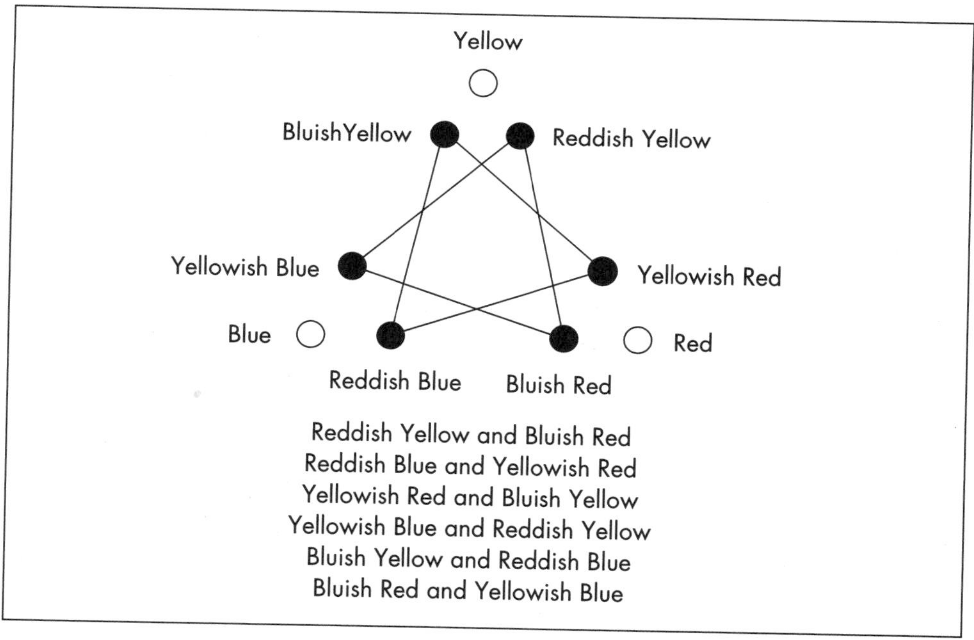

A different fundamental is the subordinate in each intermix. Each pair is located asymmetrically in relation to the two primaries that they share, one lying close to the dominant primary and the other distant from it. The effect is dissonance. Look for these colors on college penants and billboards.

RECAP: THE ARNHEIM SYNTAX OF MIXTURES

Adjacent hues are inherently:

- consonant if they lie on the same scale between two primaries;
- dissonant if they lie across the fundamental polar primary and are, therefore, from different scales; or

- dissonant if they include the polar primary.

Complementary hues are inherently:

- consonant if they share a common third hue.

Contrasting hues are inherently:

- dissonant if their subordinate hues are asymmetrical.

6.1 TYPES OF HARMONIC RELATIONSHIPS

Assemble a pair of colors to demonstrate each type of hue combination in the Arnheim syntax. These may be at whatever values and saturation levels you prefer.

Structural inversion
Similarity of the dominant
Primary with a leading tone in which it is the dominant element
Similarity of the subordinate
Primary with a leading tone in which it is the subordinate element
Structural contradiction for one common element

Do you agree that those intended to be consonant are consonant and those intended to be dissonant are dissonant? Which do you like best? Least?

6.2 ANALYSIS OF THE COLORS IN A PATTERN

Find a multicolored pattern. Analyze the color pair relationships and relate them to the Arnheim syntax of hue relationships.

What is your impression of their overall harmonic relationships—consonant, dissonant, or discordant? How do the values and saturation levels affect the harmonic relationships?

PRIMARY AND SECONDARY HUE RELATIONSHIPS

Combinations of primary and secondary hues are discussed here so that they may be compared with colors in the Arnheim syntax. Because they lack the inherent complexity and ambiguity of leading hues, pure primaries and balanced secondaries make a simpler, more primitive statement.

THE TRIAD OF PRIMARY HUES

Polar primaries paired with one another are a simple combination easily comprehended (Color Art 43*A*):

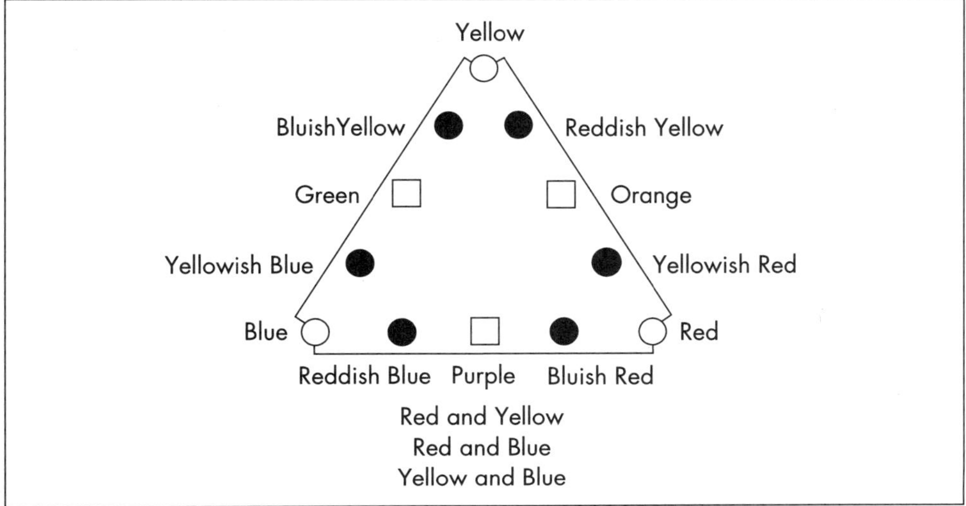

All that primary hues have in common with each other is that they are primaries; their separation from one another is absolute. Together the three balance one another.

Their simplicity makes them popular for children's toys, and delicate tints of pink and blue are traditionally associated with babies. Softened or grayed primaries are popular interior colors, as you are likely to observe on a visit to your local wallpaper or fabric store. Blue denim is a perennial favorite for casual wear.

THE TRIAD OF SECONDARY HUES

A secondary hue is more complex than a primary because it is a visually balanced intermixture of two primaries (Color Art 43C):

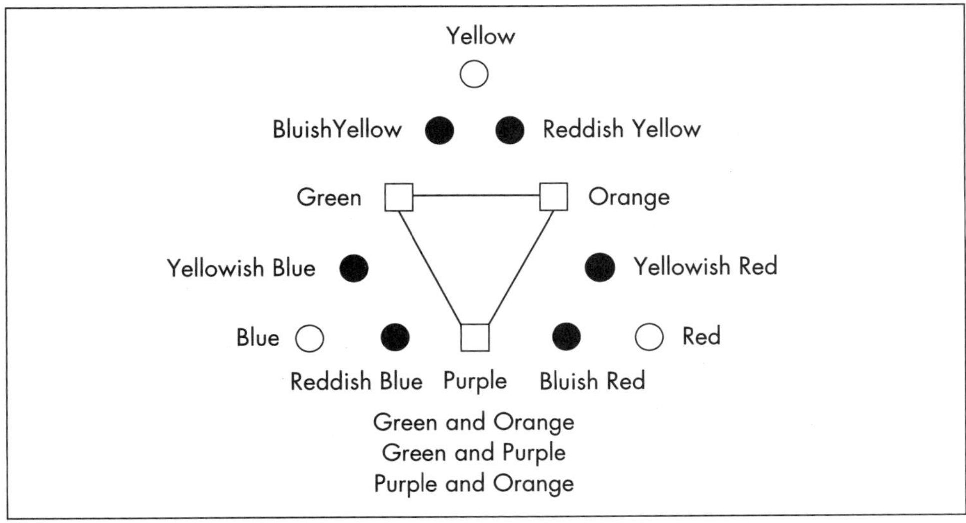

There is maximum separation between any pair of secondaries. Each secondary comes from a different scale, making two-hue combinations more dissonant than combinations of primaries. Because of their inherent complexity and dissonance, they are traditionally less frequently associated with children than are primaries.

PRIMARY–SECONDARY COMPLEMENTARIES

A primary hue and an opposite secondary hue are complementaries (Color Art 43*B*):

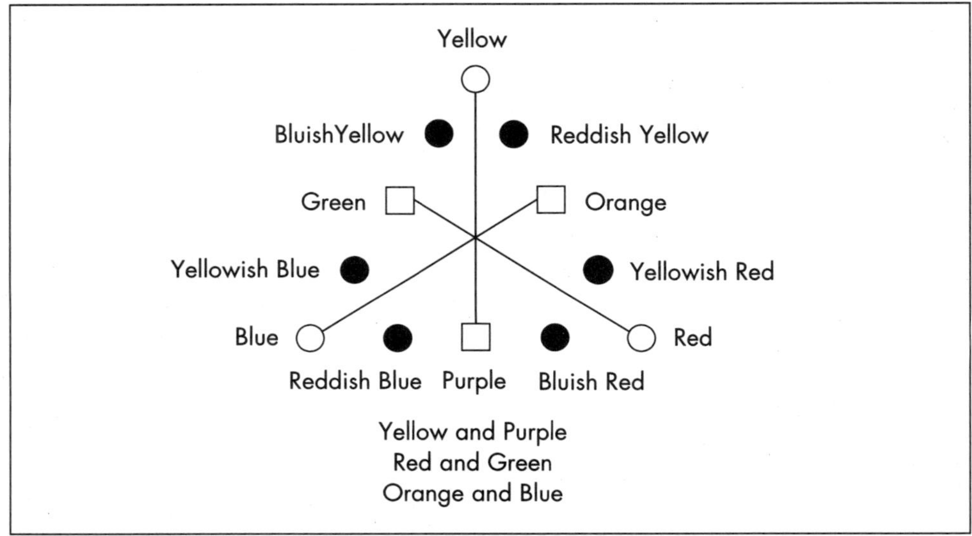

The stable primary and secondary hues are maximally different from one another and essentially unrelatable—their structural dissimilarity makes for maximum separation. Because complementary hues intensify one another, their differences are maximized.

6.3 PRIMARY AND SECONDARY HUE RELATIONSHIPS

Assemble colors that illustrate each of the primary and secondary combinations. These may be at whatever values and saturation levels you prefer.

Combinations of pure primaries
Combinations of balanced secondaries
Primary–secondary combinations

How do you like these combinations? How could you use them in an interior? Do they differ in any way from the other combinations you have assembled thus far?

HUES RELATED BY COMMON CHARACTERISTICS

Shared hues, values, or saturation levels can affect the ways that colors relate to one another.

A COMMON HUE

A hue family is a group of colors that share a common hue. The shared hue can be dominant or subordinate in any hue, but its presence is a common denominator that relates the colors to one another. The colors within the group may be consonant or dissonant.

A hue family makes a stronger statement than does an individual color. Two different hue families in a room or even within an interior complex can clash with each other and be a source of disunity. A very discriminating eye is needed if opposing color families are to coexist in the same area successfully.

As many and as diverse as the colors are in the Jack Larsen fabric (Color Art 41C), they are held together by their common yellowness. The process colors shown on the selvedge reveal that all colors are overprinted on a yellow background, which in some way comes through each color in the pattern. The dominant hues—orange, green, and purple—are dissonant, but share a common yellowness. If this fabric were placed in a dominantly red or blue room, it would clash.

COMMON VALUES AND SATURATION LEVELS

When hues are toned down or when black or white is dominant in the intermix, potency is diminished and hues' ability to clash is mitigated.

Dipping a multicolored print fabric in tea would result in somewhat neutralized blues and greens and subtly muted yellows and oranges. The shared warm neutral would serve as a common denominator, uniting colors and softening the impact of clash.

A strong dominance of white or black in the intermix of two hues can so reduce their potency that any dissonance is irrelevant. Grayness can also lessen the clash of dissonant hues, although somewhat grayed-down dissonant hues can often be unpleasant.

Extreme differences in saturation can be a source of discord. Vivid hues, in general, stand out in sharp contrast against the subdued earth tones of the natural world. Raw, pure "paint pot" vivid hues, such as cheap temperas, clash with the colors in nature, with people colors, and with other colors in an interior. The complex colors of the natural world and colors produced by vegetable dyes relate well to one another because they are low to medium in saturation and value, and reflect something of all spectral hues.

6.4 COLORS THAT SHARE COMMON CHARACTERISTICS

Assemble several colors that you consider clashing but which are united by either common blackness, whiteness, or low saturation. How does this common characteristic affect the hue relationship?

6.5 A HUE FAMILY

Select a group of colors in which each color contains some amount of a common hue. Some relationships in this combination may be consonant and others dissonant, and values and saturation levels may vary. Present as a vertical stripe composition.

How might the concept of a color family be useful? Try combining two color families in one composition. How do you like the results? Would you use them together in a room? An interior complex?

HARMONIC RELATIONSHIPS AND THE VALUES OF HUES

THE NATURAL ORDER OF HUE VALUES

At maximum saturation the various hues differ in value and, therefore, in their brightness. On a value scale of 10 to 0, in which white is 10 and black is 0, the values of hues at maximum intensity are rated as follows (Goethe as cited by De Grandis, 1986, p. 32):

- Yellow—9
- Orange—8
- Magenta—6
- Green—6
- Cyan—4
- Violet—3

This is the order in which the values of hues ordinarily occur in the natural world and the order in which we expect to see them. Yellow is almost always the lightest color you will see, and the blues, violets, and purples are usually the darkest, with other hues somewhere in the middle value range. There are exceptions, of course, such as pale lavender and pale pink flowers that are lighter than other colors in the landscape.

Moving from yellow to blue-violet on the hue circle through either the warm or the cool hues, the hues become progressively darker (Color Art 44), as from:

- yellow to yellow-green to green to cyan to blue-violet, or
- yellow to orange to red to magenta to purple.

Any combination of hues at maximum saturation in which yellow-orange appears higher in value than magenta, or green appears lighter than violet-blue, and so on, will be more consonant than if the normal value relationships are reversed.

THE NATURAL ORDER OF HUE VALUES REVERSED

If the hues become progressively lighter, moving from yellow to blue-violet through either the warm or the cool hues, the normal order of values is reversed, as in Color Art 44:

- from khaki yellow to orange to light pink to lighter magenta to still lighter lavender, or
- from khaki yellow to chartreuse to light green to lighter cyan to still lighter lavender

Where a dark mustard or khaki yellow is combined with a pale orange or pink, or a pale lavender is combined with a darker green or magenta, the expected hue values are reversed. Even if they are the same in value, a darker yellow combined with a lighter blue violet challenges the normal expectation.

Reversing the natural order of values in any pair of hues creates its own kind of dissonance, and seems to be an enduring recipe for surprise.

To reverse the natural order of values of hues in an already dissonant combination, the result may be even more unexpected, for example:

- dark khaki yellow with lighter chartreuse (a fundamental with a leading hue in which it is the dominant element), or
- a pale lavender with dark reddish brown (structural contradiction for one common element).

Did you ever wonder why there are comparatively few lavender wallpaper or fabric patterns, dishes, linens, and other items, or why lavender is so seldom seen in the work environment? Although it can be a strikingly beautiful color, lavender is dissonant with every other color.

Exotic color combinations are often sought by fashion designers, who are committed to the new and different, and reversing the expected order of values is a device that is often employed. Whether such combinations are considered beautiful, intriguing, exciting, shocking, or offensive depends on the artistry with which they are used—and, of course, the eye of the beholder.

6.6 HARMONIC RELATIONSHIPS OF HUES IN THEIR REVERSED ORDER OF VALUES

Using hues that demonstrate each of Arnheim's six categories of hue relationships, reverse the natural order of their values and create a composition in which you adjust the amounts, values, and saturation levels of the colors. Compare these colors with those in Exercise 6.1. Can you generalize about their harmonic similarities and differences?

6.7 ANALYSES OF COLOR PALETTES

Find examples of the following using photographs from catalogues, advertisements, actual samples, or the real thing:

a. A wallpaper, fabric, or rug pattern.
b. An interior photograph.
c. A painting.
d. An interior (e.g., medical office, business office, schoolroom, residence, etc.).

Using colored papers, show the relative amounts, adjacencies, and distribution of the colors. Present as a series of vertical stripes.

What types of harmonic hue relationships do you find? What types of optical interactions? In each example is there a dominant hue? A dominant value? A dominant saturation level? How do values and saturation levels affect the hues? The hue combinations?

COLOR HARMONY AND PATTERN

When a fabric or wallpaper design is printed, each color in the design requires a separate screen or roller. The process colors are usually printed on a selvedge and vary with the design.

Remember that color is a matter of perception and that *appearance color is the reality.* There may be more appearance colors than pigment colors in a composition because of the transparency of colorants and the following optical effects:

- simultaneous contrast,
- successive contrast,
- divisionist techniques, and
- overprinting, where the color underneath shows through the dye.

6.8 INCREASING THE NUMBER OF APPEARANCE COLORS

Create a three-color design that covers the entire designated area. Each color must appear as both background and foreground. The design can be a repeat pattern or a unit design. Designs may lend themselves to silk screen, block printing, or other processes.

How many appearance colors result from the various combinations? Can you identify fabrics or wallpapers that utilize this technique?

6.9 FREE STUDIES

a. Create a stripe sequence or other design using colors and color relationships that interest you.

b. Identify a color that you dislike. Combine it with other colors that give it a context in which you think it is beautiful. Present as a stripe sequence or other design.

What types of color relationships are established in each of these exercises? How would you rate each on a scale between consonant and discordant? How might they be used as interior colors? What relationships have wood tones, particularly stained woods, to other colors? What is the dominant hue in a particular wood?

COLOR HARMONY AND THE INTERIOR

Colors work the same way at interior scale as they do in a fabric or wallpaper or in the small-scale color studies that you create in the studio. In an interior, however, the areas are larger, distances between colors may be greater, and the textures of materials and illumination affect color quality.

In the interior it is easy to assess color relationships where colors come in direct contact with one another, such as a pillow on the sofa or a curtain against the wall. Colors, however, relate to one another even when located across a room from each other or in different parts of a building—they stay in the mind's eye as you divert your glance or move from one place to another. Color in one room relates harmonically to color elsewhere in the building, particularly to color in the room you are about to enter.

Interior color is experienced sequentially in space and time as you change your orientation or move through the building. Moving yourself through interesting color combinations in a complex interior can be compared to moving your eye over a painting, but the field is not static. Sequential color experiences increase the variety of harmonic relationships.

Warm, cool, dark, light, vivid, and subdued colors and neutrals can be distributed throughout an interior according to the illumination, temperature, and functional requirements of different areas of a building. The relative amounts and visual weights of colors can be apportioned, and the relationships between background, object, and accent colors can be fine-tuned. The whole can be held together by well-chosen color relationships that are based on a dominant concept.

THE DISCRIMINATING EYE

Successful color combinations require an æsthetic judgment. As useful as it may be to know whether a hue relationship is likely to be perceived as consonant or dissonant, or whether edges between colors are hard or soft, or how value and saturation levels temper hue relationships, all that this information amounts to is technique.

No technique, no formula—not even for a hue pair relationship—can substitute for the artistry of the designer. To paraphrase Duke Ellington, "If it looks good, it is good."

6.10 COLORS AND MATERIALS FOR AN INTERIOR OR AN INTERIOR COMPLEX

For an interior model of your own choosing, assemble swatches of interior materials, such as fabrics, carpet, wood, wall color or wallcovering, samples of ceramics, metals, plant materials, and the like.

a. Present these as a color-texture board.
b. Show the distribution of the colors in the model. Furniture forms may be abstracted.

What colors would you see at any one time as you move through the complex? How do the colors relate to one another both harmonically and optically? What is the dominant concept?

7 THE RELATIONSHIP BETWEEN SURFACE COLOR AND LIGHT

Because color originates in light, interior color cannot be considered apart from illumination. Color cannot be reflected off of color surfaces unless that color exists in the spectral light that illuminates it. Nor can color exist unless it is present in a surface that reflects light.

HUE IN LIGHT

Light primaries are green, orange-red, and violet-blue (Color Art 47). All other spectral hues are created by intermixing these in various proportions. Spectral color is considered additive because the light primaries combine to create white light, and white light is considered complete.

On your television screen, tiny green, orange–red, and violet–blue pixels are selectively activated to create all of the colors in the picture. White is created when all three primaries are activated, and black results when none are activated.

Secondary spectral hues are cyan, yellow, and magenta. In the sunlight spectrum, cyan is produced where violet-blue and green overlap, and yellow is produced where orange-red and green overlap. Magenta does not appear in the spectrum because violet-blue and orange-red lie at opposite ends of the band, but where these two colors of light are superimposed as in a hue circle, magenta appears where they overlap. This further demonstrates that secondary hues are produced by intermixing primary hues:

Green + Orange-red = Yellow
Orange-red + Violet-blue = Magenta
Green + Violet-blue = Cyan

SURFACE HUE

The terms surface color and pigment color are often used interchangeably. Surface colors are:

- intrinsic colors of natural materials, such as green leaves or wood or bricks, and
- pigment colors, such as those produced by paints, inks, or dyes and applied to materials.

PRIMARY, SECONDARY, AND BASIC HUES

Primary hues in pigment are magenta, cyan, and yellow (Color Art 47). All other hues can be created by intermixing these in various proportions.

Secondary pigment hues are green, violet-blue, and orange-red. Pigment secondaries are created by intermixing two pigment primaries:

Cyan + Yellow = Green
Cyan + Magenta = Violet-blue
Yellow + Magenta = Orange-red
Cyan + Yellow + Magenta = Black or Near-black

The primary and secondary hues in pigment—magenta, cyan, yellow, violet-blue, green, and orange-red—are known as the basic hues. Note that the primary hues in surface color are the secondary hues in light, and the primary hues in light are the secondary surface hues.

Surface color has three characteristics:

- Hue—warm if tinged with orange redness or cool if tinged with blueness.
- Value—high if lighter or whiter or low if darker or blacker.
- Saturation—high if vivid or full strength and lower if grayed or softened.

SURFACE HUES THAT ABSORB AND REFLECT LIGHT

Color surfaces in the environment are visible because they selectively reflect certain wavelengths light and absorb all others—the reflected hue is what you see. Because each type of illumination, whether sunlight, electric light, or firelight, has its own unique band of spectral hues, a color may appear different under different kinds of illumination. If wavelengths that correspond to a surface hue are not present in the spectrum of the light source that illuminates it, that hue does not exist—there is nothing to reflect.

Pigment or surface hue is known as subtractive because of the light it absorbs.

- If all light wavelengths are absorbed and none are reflected, black is what you see.
- If no light wavelengths are absorbed and all are reflected, white is what you see.

Surface hues are visible because of the wavelengths they selectively absorb and reflect.

- Orange-red reflects the long wavelengths and absorbs medium and short wavelengths.
- Green or yellow reflects medium wavelengths and absorbs long and short wavelengths.
- Violet-blue reflects shorter wavelengths and absorbs the medium and long wavelengths.

A color that is an intermixture of several hues will reflect each hue proportionately. If all three primaries are present in the intermixture, even in tiny amounts, the color is known as a *full-spectrum* hue.

PIGMENT PRIMARIES	LIGHT PRIMARIES REFLECTED	LIGHT PRIMARIES ABSORBED
Cyan	Violet-blue and green	Orange-red
Yellow	Green and orange-red	Violet-blue
Magenta	Orange-red and violet-blue	Green
Cyan + Yellow + Magenta	None	All

PIGMENT SECONDARIES	LIGHT PRIMARIES REFLECTED	LIGHT PRIMARIES ABSORBED
Orange-red	Orange-red	Green and violet-blue
Green	Green	Violet-blue and orange-red
Violet-blue		Orange-red and green
Orange-red + Green + Violet-blue	None	All

COMPLEMENTARY HUES

Complementary hues in pigment share no common element. In visually balanced intermixtures they neutralize one another, each absorbing the light that the other reflects, resulting in black or near-black. Smaller amounts of its complement intermixed with a hue will lower its saturation and value.

- Orange-red surface color absorbs cyan light, and cyan surface color absorbs orange-red light.
- Violet-blue surface color absorbs yellow light, and yellow surface color absorbs violet-blue light.
- Green surface color absorbs magenta light, and magenta surface color absorbs green light.

VALUE AND BRIGHTNESS

The brightness of a hue depends on the amount of light a surface reflects and absorbs. Value depends on the lightness or darkness of the pigmented surface. Value and brightness may be regarded as two sides of the same coin.

- The higher or lighter the value of a surface color, the more light it reflects and the brighter it appears.
- The lower or darker the value of a surface color, the more light it absorbs and the darker it appears.

The Munsell color solid arranges hues according to their values, with white and tints at the top changing gradually to shades and black at the bottom, corresponding to the values of the descending gray scale axis (Color Art 50).

NEUTRAL COLORS

White, gray, and black are neutral or achromatic colors. Because they have no hue, value is their only characteristic. White surface color is highest in value, reflecting all wavelengths, and black is lowest, absorbing all wavelengths. Grays range from higher to lower in value, depending on whether whiteness or blackness is dominant in the intermix.

THE VALUES OF HUES

Value is a characteristic of all surface hues (Color Art 44). Higher-value hues reflect more light; lower-value hues reflect less light.

- A *tint* is a hue lightened by intermixing it with white.
- A *shade* is a hue darkened by intermixing it with its complement or black.

Black is achieved in nature by subtracting light, not by adding black. Night is black because of the absence of light, and shadows are dark only because surfaces receive less light. The more natural way to darken a pigment hue is to subtract light from it by intermixing it with its complement. Complementary hues neutralize one another when intermixed, each darkening and reducing the saturation of the other until a visual balance produces black or near-black (Color Art 45).

SATURATION AND LIGHT

TONES OF HUES

The saturation of a hue depends on the relative amount of the specific spectral hue that a surface reflects in relation to the amount of that spectral hue that is absorbed by a toning agent.

The degree of saturation of a hue is a matter of whether it is vivid, softened, grayed, dulled, or neutralized. Saturation is sometimes referred to as *chroma,* and the degree of saturation as *chromaticity* or *tone.* Tone is a rather ambiguous term, sometimes used to indicate nuances of hue or value, but for our purposes we will use it to refer to the degree of saturation.

A high-saturation hue is brilliant and vivid, one that has not been toned down by intermixing with other pigment hues or toners. A high-saturation hue is most vivid when illuminated with light that contains an abundance of its corresponding wavelengths.

A low-saturation hue, one that is grayer, softer, duller, or more toned down, reflects less of its corresponding wavelength because more of the light that illuminates it is being absorbed by a toning agent. A pigment hue can be weakened by diluting it with a solvent or mixing it with white, but unless it has been toned down, it still remains high in saturation.

The saturation of a pigment color can be measured by comparing it to a saturation scale of that same hue at its same value level calibrated in increments between maximum vividness and neutral gray. The Munsell color solid provides such a saturation scale for each hue at each value level. Tints through shades of a hue range from high saturation on the outside through gradually lower saturation levels to gray at the center (Color Art 50).

TONING DOWN A HUE

The saturation of a hue can be reduced or toned down by the addition of a toning agent to its intermixture:

- Its complement—one hue absorbs light that the other reflects.
- Black-and-white gray—white reflects light and black absorbs it; the only hue reflected is that of the hue being toned down.
- An earth toner or earth color intermixture—light is absorbed either by a complement in the toner or by a more neutral tone.

EARTH TONES AND EARTH COLOR INTERMIXTURES

EARTH TONES

The earth tones are a large family of low-saturation colors originally derived from natural sources. They have been used throughout the ages in paints for both the exteriors and the interiors of buildings, such as the terra cotta and sienna structures associated with the Renaissance or the Mediterranean and the adobe houses of the Southwest.

They have been extensively used as toners to lower the saturation of paint hues. The most commonly used toners for interior colors include ocher or yellow oxide, raw or burnt sienna or red oxide, and raw or burnt umber.

- Sienna and ocher neutralize greens and blues.
- Umber neutralizes yellows without turning them greenish, as black is inclined to do, and is also useful for toning down the other hues.

Wood, earth, sand, brick, leather, fur, and, with very few exceptions, the skin and hair colors of most people the world over are complex, predominantly warm neutrals. For countless ages the earth tones have been the pigments with which these were represented. Used on interior surfaces, they echo people colors and relate people to the natural environment, often appearing as tints, neutrals, and off-whites.

EARTH COLOR INTERMIXTURES

Mixed earth colors are similar to their natural earth tone counterparts but are produced by intermixing secondary hues (De Grandis, 1986, p. 33) (Color Art 51):

Violet-blue + Orange-red (+ White) ⟶ Russet-brown
Orange-red + Green (+ White) ⟶ Citrine-brown
Green + Violet-blue (+ White) ⟶ Olive-brown

Earth colors vary according to which secondary is dominant in the intermix and which primary is shared by the two secondaries:

- redness in both violet and orange,
- yellowness in both orange and green, and
- blueness in both green and violet.

There can be an infinite number of gradations on the scale between any two of the parent colors, any of which may appear as tints or shades. They may be used in the same way as the earth toners, either as colors in their own right or to lower the saturation of hues.

7.1 HUE INTERMIXTURES

a. Mix every basic hue with every other basic hue. White may be added as desired. Paint a swatch of each color intermix.

Cyan	*Magenta*	*Violet-blue*
Yellow	*Orange-red*	*Green*

b. Using these swatches, create a design based on the orderly color sequence of the hue circle.

Which intermixtures change the hue? Which change the value and saturation of the hue?

7.2 EARTH COLOR INTERMIXTURES

a. *Explore the range of colors created by intermixing secondary colors with each other. Because these intermixtures are quite dark, it is necessary to add white in order to recognize the color. Paint swatches of each color intermixture.*

Violet-blue + Orange-red

Orange-red + Green

Green + Violet-blue

b. *Create a design using these colors. Other colors may be incorporated into the design.*

7.3 THE COLORS OF NATURAL MATERIALS

a. *Find 10 natural materials, such as earth, sand, stone, brick, marble, leaves, bark, wood, straw, fruits, vegetables, and so on.*
b. *Within 4-inch squares replicate in paint the colors and textures of these materials.*
   1. *Identify the dominant hue in a material and start with this color.*
   2. *Continue adding other hues, toners, and white until you can replicate the exact colors and textures of the material.*
c. *Mount the painted squares beside the original material if possible.*
d. *Compare and evaluate. What did you find out about the complexity of colors in nature?*

7.4 PEOPLE COLORS AND OTHER COLORS

a. *Mix paint swatches to match the colors of your own skin, hair, and eyes. Test the skin color match by applying a dab of paint directly to the back of your hand or your wrist.*
b. *Create a composition using the paint swatches.*
c. *Place your nature colors and people colors next to each other.*
d. *Place your people colors against backgrounds of various interior colors.*

How do the colors in part (c) relate harmonically to one another? How do the colors in part (d) relate harmonically to one another?

7.5 MIXING A "GOOD" INTERIOR BACKGROUND PAINT COLOR

Select a basic hue. Try the following combinations in various proportions:

The hue + its complement + white

The hue + an earth toner (umber, ocher, or sienna) + white

The hue + an earth color + white

The hue + black + white

Compare the colors. How are they alike? How do they differ? What can you assume about how each would appear on wall surfaces that reflect into each other?

8

INTERIOR BACKGROUND COLOR

When we speak of background color, we are often speaking of painted walls. Probably no design endeavor is as fraught with peril as predicting what a color will look like on the wall, particularly one selected from a small color chip. Theoretically, there are no "good" or "bad" colors, but you do not need an expert to tell you that some colors work well for interior background surfaces, and that others do not.

BACKGROUND COLOR IN THE HIERARCHY OF DESIGN PRIORITIES

Before wall color decisions are made, it is good to discern what role the occupant expects background color to play in the overall scheme of things.

BACKGROUND COLOR THE MOST IMPORTANT ELEMENT

Is color the interior's reason for being, its most striking feature, what you notice first on entering, and what you are most likely to comment on? If interior color is center stage, the dominant feature of the enclosure, it can provide a sense of being inside a painting, especially if color relationships change as you move from one viewing position to another. Color alone can fill the space, sometimes even compensating for innocuous structure or insignificant or minimal furnishings—or even no furniture at all.

Or it can just be a beautiful color!

Those for whom background color is the most important element in the interior will want a "good" color, interesting in its dynamic qualities and complexity, whether it is quietly neutral or more colorful. They may consider how it relates to the outside environment, to people colors, or to possessions.

COLOR AS BACKGROUND FOR PEOPLE

If the people who occupy the space and their interactions and activities are the interior's reason for being, color may or may not be an important aspect of the interior. The setting may be less important to them than the ongoing drama of their lives.

For some the background color might be ignored and the furnishings taken for granted. Even so, the general ambience of the room can still profoundly affect mood, interactions, and behavior.

For others thoughtful attention may be given to the selection of background color. It may be one that is nonintrusive and does not demand attention, but creates a comfortable and pleasant setting, or it may be one that expresses the very specific personalities and preferences of the occupants.

ARCHITECTURE THE DOMINANT FEATURE OF THE INTERIOR

Depending on your point of view, color and pattern applied to the structure either "gilds the lily" or enhances the structure. In modern buildings, white, off-white, or warm neutral are frequently used on interior wall surfaces, so that the sculptural quality of the interior architecture is articulated by the play of light, shade, and shadow. Color may be limited to furnishings, paintings, or art objects.

In some buildings, however, structural features may be emphasized by a judicious placement of color. Throughout history rich color and pattern have embellished and emphasized architectural features. Rich color, wood paneling, mosaics, murals, and the like have been integral elements that reinforce the visual structure.

In either case, the emphasis is on the architecture itself—the first thing noticed and commented upon, the star performer. In neither instance is the interior regarded as existing in order to be decorated or to provide a background for murals or other types of art.

COLOR AS BACKGROUND FOR POSSESSIONS

For some people an interior exists in order to showcase their possessions, and background colors are chosen to set off items to their best advantage. Interest derives from whatever the occupant prizes. This could be the furniture, whether antique, designer modern, or cast off; it could be the color, texture, and pattern of fabrics; it could be rugs, whether oriental or rag; it could be paintings, art objects, memorabilia with sentimental significance, trivia, or tropical fish. If furniture is top priority, the color of the wood should influence the choice of background color.

If paintings are to be emphasized, wall colors are of great significance—artists want their paintings to be displayed to optimum advantage against a favorable background color. Serious painters may disdain having their paintings regarded as decorative accessories or used to generate color schemes; nevertheless, the colors in the paintings can influence the choice of background color for the room.

UNITY AND VARIETY IN INTERIOR COLOR

Interior color choices should satisfy the need for both:

- a unifying color concept or sense of order and
- visual variety, interest, and challenge.

Order without variety can be boring and regimented, and variety without order can be chaotic and confusing.

Color can play an important role in satisfying the human need for visual variety, stimulation, and challenge. Excitement requires an element of the new and unexpected. Interesting color can alert you to your surroundings and keep you in touch with your own sensibilities; if well chosen, color can delight the eye and elevate the spirit.

Given a diversity of occupants, functions, furnishings, and expectations, color in an interior complex can be a unifying element. It can establish a sense of order and relate the parts to the whole. One is reminded of the professor's question, "Is that a 'them' or an 'it'?"

COLOR IN THE NATURAL WORLD

However remote, the natural landscape is ultimately the context within which all interior colors are experienced, whether the interior is a living, work, or play environment and whether in a rural or urban setting. The outside environment is always with us, regardless of how encased in concrete and glass we may be. We experience and accept the colors of the landscape unconsciously and without question.

The human eye has developed over millions of years in the natural world and is attuned to the colors in nature under a wide range of light conditions. Color in nature, therefore, provides a paradigm for interior color quality.

COLOR COMPLEXITY

Although no hue, value, or saturation level can automatically be declared off limits for interior use, "good" interior colors are characterized by their complexity and luminosity.

Colors in nature, such as foliage, earth, stones, and other natural materials, are complex intermixes, medium in value and medium to low in saturation. Because they contain some amount of all basic hues, they reflect some amount of all spectral hues. You become especially aware of their complexity when you mix paints to match them. The addition of its complement to a dominant color can make it a full-spectrum color, increase its complexity, and control its value and saturation.

When mixing colors to emulate the colors in nature, painters of landscapes may add a little of this color and a little of that until a desired balance is struck—a process sometimes referred to as color loading. The end results are ultimately the same as intermixing the three primaries but using a more diverse palette. The trained eye can discern the individual component hues included in such an intermix. This might be compared to the ability to taste the separate ingredients in a cake—the sugar, butter, flour, egg, vanilla, and so on—or the ability to distinguish all of the notes in a music chord.

Nature is sparing in its use of brilliant color, limiting it to vivid accents such as flowers and birds or to brief periods of time such as sunsets and in autumn leaves or crocuses in spring. Even the most brilliant cardinal, autumn leaf, or sunset, however, never approaches a pure "paint pot" red, foliage is never a vivid green, and an orange is never a vivid orange in color.

It should be noted that, as beautiful as color pack colors are, few are interior background colors, most of them lacking the subtlety generally desired for wall surfaces. You may wish to make your own comparison of interior paint color samples with the color pack colors.

LUMINOSITY

Luminosity has to do with the quality of light reflected from a surface, penetrating it, or transmitted through it.

Filtered Light

When light is filtered through the red and yellow leaves of a maple in the fall or through a chintz curtain or through the stained glass of a cathedral, their colors are brighter or more luminous than when light is merely reflected from their surfaces. The colors become higher in value and more highly saturated.

Light That Penetrates

When light penetrates the surface of an "old master" painting, it is reflected from several layers of transparent colors. Light is reflected back and forth within the finish and outward from the several layers of the finish as well. Colors assume greater depth and richness than when light is merely reflected from the outer surface. Layers of clear lacquer on antique furniture enrich the colors of the wood in a comparable manner. The surfaces of leaves and flowers are lustrous, as light penetrates their surfaces and is reflected outward from several levels.

Transparent colorants in interior wall paints can create a similar effect. They can impart greater depth and luminosity to wall surfaces than opaque paints that reflect light only from the outer surface.

When the textures of stone, brick, or matte paints are illuminated, small shadows and highlights on their surfaces reveal their textural depth. Velvet achieves its luster from the complex way it reflects light, some light penetrating the pile, other light being reflected from the surface.

Reflected Light

Because colors in the natural world are full-spectrum hues, they respond to changes in the light during different weather conditions and according to the time of day. Interior colors are also more responsive to varying light conditions if they include even tiny amounts of the basic hues in their intermixes. This enables them to reflect more readily the cool tones of a cloudy day and the warm tones of a pink sunset than if the paints contained only one hue ingredient.

Luminosity of interior background colors is a subtle phenomenon, more evident when you are surrounded by a color than when viewing a small sample. Reflected light from an interior surface color seems to permeate the space; you do not ordinarily refer to an interior as a room with blue walls—you are more likely to speak of it as a blue room.

CHARACTERISTICS OF COLORS

The kind and amount of energy that color imparts to the interior evokes some type of feeling response—it can calm or stimulate, soothe or exhilarate, cheer or depress. There are many words with which you can describe the effects of interior color.

Nor is there any shortage of opinions about what generic hues on interior background surfaces are supposed to do, or how they affect your work, or what you are supposed to think of them, or how they make you feel. Often these assessments ignore the fact that the slightest modification in the value or saturation of a hue, the complexity of its intermix, or its interaction with other colors can bring about vast differences in color meaning and dynamics. Yet some general conclusions may be drawn regarding how generic hues are experienced in interior spaces.

HUES

Reds

Reds are generally regarded as stimulating and exciting. They are thought to speed up heart and respiration rates and to raise blood pressure, and they are associated with strength, passion, and the color of blood and fire (Bloomer, 1976, p. 120). Pure fundamental red is the color of the carpet rolled out for a celebrity.

Orange-red, the hottest color, is like glowing embers—the more vivid, the hotter it is, and the more energy it brings to an interior. When intermixed with other hues, it gives them warmth. Although highly advancing when highly saturated, lower saturation tints of orange-red can bring a glow of warmth to an interior, yet recede. Cedar paneling, for instance, is a low-saturation reddish orange that approaches brown, and because of its complexity it can be very rich. A low-saturation pure red is popular but lacks the complexity of an intermix. In some low-saturation tones, it can be depressing as an interior background color.

In a controlled experiment Kwallek and Lewis assessed the effect of a red versus a green versus a white office environment on worker productivity and mood. It was predicted that those who worked in the red office would find it a more tense environment and would make more errors. The workers in the red office, however, actually made fewer errors than those in the white or green offices, even though they found the color distracting (Kwallek and Lewis, 1980, p. 275).

Blues

Blues are considered calming, restful, serene, cool, comfortable, sober, and contemplative. They suggest dignity, poise, and reserve (Sharpe, 1974, p. 91). They are thought to reduce blood pressure, pulse, and respiration rates (Bloomer, 1976, p. 120; Mahnke and Mahnke, 1993, p. 13). Perhaps this is because blue occurs so frequently at medium or low saturation, for example, denim blue. Some blues, however, can also be considered frightening, depressing, melancholy, and cold (Mahnke and Mahnke, 1993, p. 13).

Although blue is generally regarded as receding, a high saturation "electric" blue can advance quite strongly, and be neither calming nor contemplative but quite the opposite. Mahnke and Mahnke (1993) consider the greener blues, presumably cyan, easier to use in interiors than a fundamental blue, reaffirming the greater appeal of the complex intermix over the pure fundamental hue.

Greens

In green areas of the world, green is the background color, and all colors are seen within a green context. In this regard it may be considered a neutral. Green is both warm and cool; it contains both the calming presence of blueness and the energy of yellowness; its blueness suggests shadow, whereas its yellowness suggests light. Low saturation greens can serve as a transition between architecture and nature (Kaufman and Dahl, 1992, p. 130).

Mahnke and Mahnke consider green to be retiring, relaxing, tranquil, refreshing, quiet, and natural, although it can also be common, tiresome, and associated with guilt. It is associated with the power of nature and of life, particularly plant life, yet some greens are also associated with decay and nausea (Mahnke and Mahnke, 1993, pp. 12–13).

In the Kwallek and Lewis experiment, it was predicted that subjects working in the green office would perform better than those in the red office. No significant difference was found, however, between the productivity of those working in the two offices (Kwallek and Lewis, 1980, p. 276).

Yellows

Yellows are considered sunny, cheerful, and high spirited, the happiest of all colors (Mahnke and Mahnke, 1993, p. 12) (Color Art 52 and 53). Yellow is expansive—it appears to spread out as well as to advance (Swirnoff, 1988, p. 38). Children portray yellow as the color of the sun, the source of light, and as the color of light it seems to illuminate the space. At maximum saturation it is the most aggressive of the hues.

Yellow is thought to be unflattering to some people, in that it can make a sallow complexion appear more sallow and can emphasize blue circles around the eyes.

Purples and Violets

Purple, a mixture of red and blue, can evoke delicacy and richness or appear unsettling and degenerate. It is considered dignified, exclusive, but lonely, mournful, or pompous (Mahnke and Mahnke, 1993, p. 13).

Violet-blue, normally the darkest of all the hues, has great richness and depth at maximum saturation and is associated with dignity, wealth, majesty, and splendor. At higher values and medium to low saturation, it is the most ephemeral and least tangible of all colors, a mystical color evoked by shadows and twilight. In the presence of yellow, its complement, it assumes a stronger identity. (Bloomer, 1976, p. 120; Kaufman and Dahl, 1992, p. 223). Pale tints of purples and violets are more light hearted, but because they are dissonant with other hues, they can be problematic in the interior environment.

VALUES

Whites and Off-Whites

Pure white is white at its maximum strength, uncontaminated with any other color. With no transition ingredient to soften its impact or to relate it to other colors, to people, or to the environment, it is neutral, bold, assertive, and inclined toward coldness. At full strength pure white makes an extremely strong statement, and provides value contrast with other colors.

White may be softened by the addition of a toner, each toner imparting its own characteristic to it. An earth toner gives it warmth, a dash of black imparts a cool grayness, and complementary hues and earth colors increase its complexity. A complex white picks up hues reflected from other surfaces more readily and is also more responsive to differences in spectral light, such as the coolness of a northern exposure or the warmth of a sunset.

The dominance of one hue in a white intermix can emphasize either warmth or coolness and may be experienced more as an aura than as a hue. Any paint company's samples will include a wide variety of whites—whites inclined toward pinkness, yellowness, blueness, and so on. The quality of light entering the room, however, makes the greater difference.

Kwallek and Lewis found that subjects working in a white office made more errors than those working in a red or a green office. They liked working in a white environment, however, and considered it to be a more appropriate color for an office than either red or green (Kwallek and Lewis, 1980, p. 277).

Although whites and off-whites are often avoided because they show soil easily, off-whites are used extensively in rental properties because they are calculated not to clash with whatever colors the tenants' furnishings may be.

Off-whites are popular for interior use because of their light airiness; but whether any white is regarded as airy and light or as "dead white"—stark and sterile—may lie in the eye of the beholder. Mahnke and Mahnke regard white as static, boring, and tedious, not providing adequate sensory stimulation, especially in institutional settings, such as hospitals and homes for the elderly (Mahnke and Mahnke, 1993, pp. 23–24). They suggest that white is "touch inhibiting, that white floors discourage being walked on (Mahnke and Mahnke, 1993, p. 16).

Both Birren and Mahnke and Mahnke regard off-whites to be as undesirable as pure white. Birren warns against the use of whites in high-brightness areas, especially where glare is a problem or where the general field is bright but the task to be performed is dimly lit (Birren, 1978, p. 39). "High environmental brightness not only handicaps seeing...but also severely constricts the pupil opening of the human eye, an action that is muscular and very fatiguing" (Birren, 1978, p. 105).

Obviously, whites should be used with care and only if suitable for the area and the client. Highly reflective white surfaces and poor control of the light can create problems, especially for those with impaired vision.

Tints

A tint contains a somewhat larger proportion of a hue or neutral in its white base than does an off-white. Tinted walls can infuse color into the interior while maintaining high light reflectance. Because of the quantity of color they bring to an interior and because of surfaces reflecting into one another, tints can be as powerful as smaller amounts of strong color, such as in a painting or on a single colored wall.

White dilutes a hue but does not tone it down. Regardless of the amount of white in the intermix, the hue remains saturated until grayed or softened. Although pale, high-saturation tints can have a lively, fresh quality, somewhat stronger tints on wall surfaces can appear gaudy or even vulgar (e.g., "pink, paink, or punk," as described by a wag). Tints of basic or leading hues are more complex than tints of fundamental hues, and are generally, although not always, to be preferred. Grayed tints can sometimes impart a quality of mistiness to a room.

Because of the sometime association of light tints with weak sentiment, they may be considered inappropriate for some uses, such as a bank lobby or the men's locker room. Complex, toned-down tints can be more substantial, yet maintain high light reflectance in an interior, the critical factor being its complexity.

Shades

At maximum saturation violet-blue or purple pigments can be so black that white must be added to them to make the hue apparent. Shades of middle- and high-value hues are created by intermixing the hues with a toner, usually the complement or perhaps black. Dark shades of yellow or yellow-dominant intermixtures lose the essence of their yellowness.

Any deep color is livelier and more luminous with the presence of even an infinitesimal amount of its complement in the intermix. Darkened hues can be incredibly rich on interior wall surfaces. They may be whitened somewhat and still be considered shades, although whitening them might produce a chalky appearance, which may not be desired. Dark low-saturation hues as well as brighter dark hues can be an effective foil for brilliant accent hues and whites.

The amount of dark wall surface may need to be limited unless the sense of an enveloping enclosure is desired or unless the space is well illuminated. When used on an individual wall or as an accent color in an otherwise neutral interior, the value contrast can produce dramatic effects. Because dark colors absorb so much light, they need brighter illumination than do colors of higher value.

TONES

Vivid Hues

Vivid hues on interior surfaces can be dramatic and daring, have maximum impact, and impart maximum energy to a room. Contrary to popular belief, vivid hues do not have to be overpowering when used skillfully and in the right place. It goes without saying, however, that some high-saturation hues are more successful for interior use than others. The distinction must be made between the raw, "paint pot" colors of cheap temperas, for instance, and the more sophisticated high saturation colors manufactured for interior use.

Magenta in interior paint never quite seems to equal orange red in brilliance. Red created by intermixing orange red and magenta is more complex than pure primary red, as orangeness in orange-red interacts with blueness in magenta, thereby providing a subtle softening effect. Both orangeness and blueness may be discerned in the color, depending on the lighting conditions.

Even though yellow is associated with light, pure, undiluted "paint pot" chrome yellow can appear heavy and aggressive on any surface. Yellow can be substantially reduced in saturation and still appear quite vivid.

The brilliance of greens, blues, purples, and magentas of Thai silks and Christmas ornaments cannot be replicated in paint. The colors can be reproduced, but the textures that give the colors their luster cannot. However, with the use of transparent colorants and skillful adjacencies, the effects of brilliance can be emulated.

Clear Tones

The difference between a clear tone and one of higher or lower saturation is a matter of degree and the eye of the beholder. A clear tone is somewhat softer than a full-saturation "paint pot" hue. It may be high or low in value, but its saturation is slightly reduced.

Clear tones can be cheerful, stimulating, invigorating, and can bring to the room high energy. In comparison with high-saturation hues that can seem ferociously aggressive, clear tones are more likely to enliven the interior without being overly assertive. Clear tones make a strong statement, and the amount of strong color in an area should be determined by the amount of stimulation desired for the space, the illumination, and user preferences.

Tones of Medium or Lower Saturation

It is almost an axiom that interior surface colors should be toned down so that they will "lie flat on the wall" or "not stick out like a sore thumb." Most interior colors are tones of medium or lower saturation. Soft, beautiful colors are popular because they do not impose themselves too strongly on the observer. They can complement people colors, and make excellent backgrounds.

Although the low-saturation hues can be among the most beautiful interior colors, they also risk being innocuous, especially if they are associated with bland and boring floral patterns in complementary or contrasting hues and with little or no value contrast. Often they are the choice of those who want some color but are afraid of it.

Warm Neutrals

The popularity of beige, warm grays, and off-whites at high or medium value attests to the almost unanimous desire for nonintrusive backgrounds. Neutrals do not call attention to themselves and can easily be taken for granted, permitting the attention to be concentrated on people and activities. In high values they impart the airiness and spaciousness of white to an interior.

Wood paneling, whether in familiar or exotic woods, or weathered wood can suggest "back to nature," lending warmth even to sophisticated urban settings. Quiet dignity and restraint are conveyed by the soft color of the wood, the rich fabrics and carpeting, 18th-century detailing, and low lighting in the showroom depected in Color Art 55. Dark full-spectrum earth colors can provide rich neutral backgrounds, their warmth or coolness depending on which ingredient hues are dominant in the intermix.

Depressing grayness or brownness and the lack of hue characterize slums and run-down properties, even though the same grays and browns in more prosperous settings might be considered beautiful. Background color is only one aspect of an environment, but its association with poverty and grime affects the meanings attributed to it.

Grays

Depending on viewer bias and the skill with which they are used, achromatic black-and-white gray backgrounds can be regarded as conservative, sophisticated, calming, or depressing. They permit attention to be focused on furnishings or people, although they do little or nothing to enhance people or environment colors. Black-and-white grays are an effective foil for the brighter colors that people wear, for colorful furnishings or art objects, or for luxurious textures, especially where texture is the dominant element of interest.

Grays can be light or dark, warm or cool, depending on the black–white balance and the presence of hue in the intermix. Any paint company's color chips will include both warm and cool grays ranging from cool bluish, greenish, violetish, and purplish grays to warm or pinkish grays to grays tinged with yellow, orange, or brown overtones—all in a wide range of values.

Grays produced by balanced mixtures of complements and white are more complex, differing from one another as the hue components differ. Where complex grays created by different pairs of complements are juxtaposed with one another or with a black-and-white gray, their differences become obvious.

Grays in the interior surround need value contrast. Middle- to low-value gray combined with middle- to low-value, low-saturation hues can be exceptionally boring. For several years dull red, dull green, and gray have been fashionable colors for restaurants, medical facilities, and other public places, as though smog had settled over the scene. Without the relief of value and saturation contrast, such colors can be exceptionally uninteresting, especially in fundamental primary hues and plastic.

Blacks

Pure black walls are more likely to be seen in the media and in furniture showrooms than in residential settings—black is seldom used architecturally except perhaps as accent trim. In combination with other colors, blacks may be compared to the bass notes of a musical scale, often providing needed value contrast.

Off-blacks are frequently found camouflaging structural beams and ducts and lowering the apparent heights of ceilings in commercial buildings, such as converted warehouses, discotheques, restaurants, showrooms, and the like.

Black or near-black walls close in on you like the night. They can suggest intimacy, enclosure, mystery, seduction, or may be considered threatening or depressing unless relieved by contrast or lots of windows.

Window areas are black at night and should be curtained if the blackness is found objectionable.

TONING AGENTS

Complements

Complementary hues neutralize one another and in balanced intermixtures produce black or near-black. The addition of its complement to the intermix darkens a hue, whereas the addition of its complement plus white reduces its saturation. White is used to control the value.

A hue plus its complement creates a full-spectrum hue and is, therefore, the preferred means of reducing saturation or value.

Black-and-White Grays

Adding black to a hue darkens it, and adding black-and-white gray to a hue lowers its saturation. White is used to raise the value. The relative proportions of the hue, black, and white determine whether the color is a grayed hue or a hued gray.

Because black-and-white gray contributes no hue to an intermix, white reflecting all spectral hues and black absorbing them, the only spectral wavelengths reflected are those of the hue itself. Gray, therefore, contributes nothing to the complexity of a hue. "Pure colors mixed with white, gray, or black suffer a deterioration of hue, which becomes pale, opaque, or dull respectively—in any event the color always appears weaker, never brighter" (De Grandis, 1986, p. 41).

Earth Toners and Earth Color Intermixtures

Throughout the ages color has been sought among earth materials or anywhere it could be found. Earth toners—the umbers, ochers, siennas—are frequently used today by paint manufacturers for mixing neutrals and for reducing the saturation and increasing the complexity of interior colors. Being opaque, they have good covering ability but little luminosity (Kaufman and Dahl, 1992, p. 216).

Earth color intermixtures can be used to tone down hues in the same way as the earth toners, but with a wide range of possibilities because of the wide variety of colors that combinations of secondary hues can produce. Used as toners, they can transform a hue into a full spectrum color. Light is reflected not only from the dominant hue, itself, but also from the hue components in the toner.

INTERIOR PAINTS

There are three ways to obtain interior paint colors:

- purchase a custom-mixed color,
- alter a custom-mixed color, or
- mix it yourself.

COMMERCIAL PAINT COLOR SYSTEMS

The Custom-Mixed Color Palette

When you shop for a custom-mixed paint color, you find the paint manufacturer's color collections attractively arranged in a display case. The arrangement facilitates comparisons and offers a wide variety of choices.

These collections often include thousands of color choices shown on color cards. Colors in various tints and shades are computer coded, evenly spaced, and notated, and within each group you can find hues ranging from clear to muted and related near-neutrals. The colors chosen for display represent the manufacturer's and the color stylist/consultant's reading of future trends (Linton, 1994, pp. 175–177).

Colorants

Paint manufacturers have carefully selected palettes of colorants from which their custom-mixed colors are produced. Because each paint company has its own colorants, the colors that one company mixes are likely to differ subtly from those mixed by another company, making it difficult to match exactly a hue of one brand with the hue of another brand.

In a sampling of paint stores the following colorants were found to be used for custom-mixing interior colors:

Benjamin Moore: Yellow, yellow oxide (ocher), red oxide, black, bright blue, thalo green, magenta, clear red, orange, gray.

Bruning: Red, blue, black, raw umber, yellow oxide, brown, red oxide, green, violet, yellow, medium yellow.

Devoe and Raynolds: Nonbleeding yellow, permanent yellow, yellow, thalo green, thalo blue, red iron oxide, permanent orange, fast red, violet, brown iron oxide, umber, yellow oxide, magenta, white extender, lamp black.

Duron: Lemon yellow, black, yellow oxide, thalo green, thalo blue, red oxide, fast red (true red), iron oxide, violet, raw umber, orange.

Glidden: Yellow oxide, thalo blue, fast red, red oxide, thalo green, magenta, lemon fast yellow, white, black.

Martin Senour: Gold (sienna), blue, red, maroon, yellow, violet, black, green, white, umber.

Pratt and Lambert: Blue, orange, violet, black, brown, green, deep red, bright red, bright yellow, deep yellow.

Sherwin Williams: Red, green, yellow, blue, violet, yellow oxide (deep gold), red oxide (maroon, not sienna), raw umber, black.

Earth toners from the preceding list are yellow oxide (ocher), red oxide (sienna), iron oxide, gold, raw umber, brown or brown oxide, gray, and black.

GETTING THE COLOR YOU WANT

THE CUSTOM-MIXED COLOR

At the paint store you can learn the recipe of a custom-mixed color, and it may be exactly the color you want. The hue has been toned down with its complement or missing primaries, and there may even be traces of additional hues in the intermixture.

ALTERING A CUSTOM-MIXED COLOR

If, however, the custom-mixed color is not of the color or the complexity you want, additional colorant can be added. Values and intensities of custom-mixed hues are often reduced with opaque black-and-white grays or opaque earth toners. These pigments make colors that are easy to match, but the colors lack the complexity of those toned down by their complements or missing primaries (Kaufman and Dahl, 1992, p. 216).

Some commercial stains used to enhance the color of wood are harsh orange or red tones that lack the subtlety of natural wood tones. Such stains can also be toned down by adding a small amount of the complement or other colorants to the intermix.

The addition of even a tiny amount of a missing primary or secondary hue or earth color to a paint color can complete the range of spectral hues reflected. If maintaining vividness is desired, the amount of the toning agent can be miniscule.

Additional colorants may be added at the paint store using the increment dispenser (Kaufman and Dahl, 1992, p. 218).

MIXING YOUR OWN COLOR

Colorants should be added to the appropriate tinting base, and because interior color is usually required in quantity, it should be mixed by the gallon. If more than one gallon is to be mixed, it is necessary to measure carefully and record the amounts of colorants used (Kaufman and Dahl, 1992, p. 217).

When paint colors are to be created in quantity, there are two ways to test a color match:

- adding a small amount of a wet paint mixture to another wet paint mixture for comparison, and
- comparing the colors when they are dry.

Only when a paint is dry can its true color be ascertained.

When mixing tints, it is helpful to remember the example of the drop of ink in a gallon of water versus the drop of water in a gallon of ink. A small amount of a colorant added to a larger quantity of white base produces a far more noticeable difference than a small amount of white added to a larger quantity of a colorant.

When mixing paint colors, it is necessary to proceed cautiously and to test the colors frequently.

TRANSPARENCY VERSUS THE COVERING ABILITY OF PAINTS

A paint's ability to cover must be taken into account, and several coats may be needed in order to cover the surface properly. Transparent colorants do not cover as well as those that are opaque—white has better covering ability than some colors.

One layer of paint color applied to a white surface produces maximum vividness, because the light penetrates to the underlying white that reflects all colors and is reflected back through the color. As additional layers of paint are applied, the density of the color will be increased but not its intensity. "Thick applications of paint prevent the incident rays from penetrating all the layers and therefore from being reflected back. The more layers or the more opaque the paint, the less vibrant and the darker the color becomes" (De Grandis, 1984, pp. 42-43).

METAMERISM

Two colors that appear the same under one light but differ under another are known as *metamers*. Under one type of illumination, a color toned down with a black-and-white gray may appear to match exactly the same color toned down with its complement. Under another type of illumination, however, the two intermixtures will not match, because the different colorants reflect different wavelengths in spectral light. It may be difficult to match exactly a color made by one manufacturer with a color made by another, because they may not be using exactly the same colorants.

This has been a major problem for the furnishings and building industries as well as individuals who wish to match paint colors, but color matching can now be facilitated by computer. The computer can analyze a paint sample according to the component hues in the intermixture and recommend exactly which hue ingredients will replicate the original. This should make it easier to match one brand of paint color with another.

TYPES OF INTERIOR PAINTS

COMPOSITION

Paint technology has continued to improve interior paints both in ease of application and in durability.

- Latex paints are the most widely used for interior wall surfaces. Latex is a synthetic resin used in making water-thinned paints.
- Acrylic paints differ from latex in the type of resin they contain and are presumed to hold color better.
- Alkyd paints are oil-based paints that contain alkyd resins and are thinned with paint thinner or mineral spirits. They dry to a harder film and have better color retention than latex paints.

LIGHT REFLECTION

Interior paints come in a variety of textures ranging from flat to high gloss.

- Flat paint has a dull, matte surface that scatters the light and gives it a soft appearance.
- Semigloss paint has a medium gloss. It is easy to clean and is popular for woodwork or kitchens.
- High-gloss paints produce glossy surfaces that are highly reflective and can produce glare when illuminated from certain angles. They are the most soil and stain resistant and the easiest to clean of all paint surfaces.

Any paint with a hard finish, regardless of sheen, may be considered an enamel. The higher the proportion of resin content, the greater the film toughness. Enamels are available in:

- flat, low luster,
- eggshell or satin finish,
- semigloss, and
- high gloss.

PAINT BASES

Paint colors are obtained by mixing the colorant into a paint base or carrier appropriate to the saturation and value of the color. A white or titanium base is used for mixing tints. Vivid and darker colors require greater amounts of pigment, so the bases for these contain less and less white. The bases for very deep, dark colors have no white. Dark colors are less durable, especially in flat paints, and may mark easily or even rub off.

Different paint companies call their base colors by various names but essentially they are:

- white base—for tints
- pastel base—will hold 4 ounces of colorant per gallon
- intermediate or midtone—will hold 6 to 8 ounces of colorant per gallon
- deep base or deep tone—less body; will hold 8 to 12 ounces of colorant per gallon
- accent base or ultra deep tone—for vivid colors

TESTING COLOR CHOICES

The only way to be sure how a paint color will appear in a room is to paint the entire room, furnish it, and illuminate it. This subjects the color to the exact lighting conditions under which it will be viewed and makes it possible to observe the dynamics of the color in the space. If the color turns out to be undesirable, the room must be repainted. This is not a preferred method for validating color choices, but it happens often enough, even to experienced designers. (I never did find out who paid to have a hall, staircase, living room, and dining room repainted, when the expert colorist with years of experience announced that the new color throughout was absolutely the wrong green.)

Although paint is probably one of the less costly sources of color in an interior, the error in trial and error can be an expensive and time-consuming nuisance for a small room and out of the question for large complexes. Some type of testing should always precede the painting of an interior surface:

- The sample board—shows harmonic relationships among swatches of colors and materials, but the question of color dynamics within the enclosure is not addressed.
- Large samples of the colors—a quart of paint, a 4-foot x 6-foot wall board, and a 3-yard length of fabric can be a worthwhile investment.
- An interior model—this enables you to observe the effects of ambient light on color surfaces.
- A mock-up of the room under the light that will illuminate the colors.

Your best bet for developing the ability to predict "good" interior background color is your own background knowledge of color composition and color dynamics and your experience using real color in real enclosures. Understanding, observation, awareness, and an eye for color underlie the ability to make quick, decisive, and successful interior color choices. This can be a lifetime pursuit.

8.1 COLOR FOR AN INTERIOR MODEL

a. *Assemble on a sample board swatches of upholstery, window treatments, and any other significant color materials for a room. Use these selections as a basis for the colors in three identical one-room models of a room of your own choosing.*

b. *Mix colors for the floor, wall, and ceiling surfaces for the three models based on the materials you have chosen:*

   Model 1—a tint or soft tone dominant
   Model 2—a clear tone dominant
   Model 3—a dark shade dominant

c. *Mix colors for objects and other surfaces in the room. Cubes may be used to indicate furniture. The dominant color of a patterned fabric, wallcovering, or rug may be shown as a solid color.*

Which model do you like best? Least? Do the colors appear the way you had envisioned them? How do the three types of color affect the spatial qualities of the interiors? What happens to the colors in the light? How do the colors relate to colors in the landscape? To the furnishings? To people colors?

8.2 COLOR FOR A FULL-SCALE ROOM

Paint the wall and ceiling surfaces of a room using either:

a. a custom-mixed color,
b. an altered custom-mixed color, or
c. a color you mix from "scratch."

Do you consider the colors successful or not? Are the results what you expected? Which do you prefer? What, if anything, would you change? Do the colors advance or recede? Does the room appear larger or smaller than before it was painted? If more than one surface color was used throughout, how have the visual proportions of the room been modified? How do the colors interact with people colors? With environment colors? With each other, both optically and harmonically?

9 ILLUMINATION, REFLECTIVE MATERIALS, AND COLOR

Because there can be no color without light and because light remains invisible until it is reflected by a surface, all interior color decisions involve illumination and the textures of materials.

Each interior is unique because of variability in both the light conditions and the reflective qualities of materials. Interactions between color, light, and materials make predicting how any color will appear on an interior surface a risky undertaking at best. Color decisions, therefore, cannot be based on formulas or rigid guidelines; ultimately, they are a matter of the designer's intuition based on skill and experience.

DAYLIGHT

Surface colors as they appear in daylight are considered to be the "true" colors, yet daylight conditions are not constant. Daylight is primarily cool, but the daylight spectrum is subject to great warm-to-cool fluctuations because of atmospheric and weather conditions, time of day, season, geography, orientation, and the changing angles at which sunlight penetrates the atmosphere.

Daylight results from the refraction and reflection of sunlight by small atmospheric particles of moisture or dust suspended in the atmosphere. When skies are clear most of the light comes through; however, these minute particles color the atmosphere and make the sky a source of diffuse or ambient light.

On a cloudy day larger water particles refract and reflect all wavelengths equally, making the sky appear white (Moore, 1986, pp. 31–32). There is only diffuse daylight with a dominance of blue wavelengths.

At sunset the sun has to penetrate the atmosphere at a low angle, where the greater density of the atmosphere causes all but the longest wavelengths to be scattered, and that is why sunsets are red (Kuehni, 1983, pp. 19–20).

BRIGHTNESS IN THE DAYLIT INTERIOR

Radiant light from the sun enters the interior as:

- daylight or diffuse light from the sky, or
- direct sunlight.

The hue, value, and saturation of a color are all affected by the amount and type of light that illuminates it.

DIFFUSE DAYLIGHT

Daylight in the interior produces a soft, nondirectional, relatively shadow-free illumination, often referred to as general lighting. Daylight reaches into far corners and illuminates shade and shadow areas. We see objects and surfaces because the light that they reflect conveys information about them (Gibson, 1979, p. 51).

Outdoor light conditions seem to be exaggerated indoors. Especially during stormy weather it seems darker inside than out.

Tall trees and tall buildings can obstruct light from entering an interior, whereas unobstructed openings into the interior and reflective surfaces outside serve to brighten it.

DIRECT SUNLIGHT

Patches of Sunlight

Direct sunlight enters an interior through windows and doors at an oblique angle, creating brilliantly lit patches of light in fantastic shapes. As the sun moves across the sky, these light patches move across floors, walls, and objects and contrast sharply in brightness with the darker shadow areas next to them. As stated by Moore, "The movement and sparkle associated with controlled shafts of sunlight add considerably to the visual variety and excitement of space" (Moore, 1986, p. 30).

Shadow

A shadow is cast where an obstruction prevents direct light from falling on a surface. Shadows, therefore, occur only against directly lit surfaces. Shadows of paned windows, plants, blinds, or other objects create patterns as complex as the patches of sunlight themselves, and together they enliven the surfaces on which they fall.

Shadows subtract light and differ in degree of brightness. In strong light shadows are distinct, as simultaneous contrast exaggerates both the brightness of the lighted area and the darkness of the shadow against which it is seen. The brighter the light, the darker the shadow appears. In diffuse light shadows may be nonexistent or poorly defined. Look carefully at shadows cast by diffuse light and observe the degree to which they are evident.

Shade

Shade areas occur where the sun cannot reach and are lit by ambient light reflected from other surfaces. In diffuse light you may not be able to distinguish shade areas from shadow. Shade is seldom as dark as a shadow cast on a bright patch of sunlight, and may appear brighter on surfaces near door and window openings.

Glare

Glare is excess light coming from the wrong direction (Gordon and Nuckolls, 1995, p. 35).

Reflected glare is produced when the angle of vision is the same as the angle of the light source, as when sunlight is reflected from water or snow. Reflected glare can be dazzlingly bright and can make even the darkest of colors appear white with a brilliance painful to the eyes. Glare can be generated from inside the interior by light reflected off a shiny surface, such as a metallic wallpaper, glass, a polished floor, or a high gloss enamel.

Direct glare is experienced where a bare light bulb shines in your eyes or where bright light enters a dark room through a small window.

LIGHT REFLECTANCE OF INTERIOR SURFACES

DIFFERENTIAL ILLUMINATION

If all interior surfaces were the same color and texture and received the same amount of light, they would be indistinguishable from one another. The effect would not only be very boring, it would be totally disorienting.

In the 1970s James Turrell became known for installations of "rooms" in art galleries around the country. These "rooms" were painted light gray and lighted so that on entering them no distinction could be made between one surface and another, and no corners were visible. The experience was like being in a fog.

9.1 ELIMINATING BRIGHTNESS DIFFERENCES WITHIN A MODEL

a. Find or make a model that is open at the front and has a ceiling with an opening to admit light. Place it under a lamp so that the light enters through the ceiling opening to create patches of direct light, shadows, and shade areas in the interior.
b. Paint the interior or the object background with shades and tints of gray so that all surfaces appear to be the same value, with no visible differences between direct light, shadow, and shade areas.

Or:

a. Place an object in front of a light gray or white background and illuminate it so that there are shadows within the object and on the background.
b. Paint the object and the background so that both are the same hue and value and no shadow is apparent.

What does this tell you about the effect of brightness differences on environment legibility? On hue?

The architectural interior is actually a light modulator. No two surfaces can be identical in color, because each surface receives and reflects daylight differently.

The amount and intensity of daylight normally falls on interior surfaces in the following order from most to least:

- the floor,
- a wall facing the light source,
- a wall perpendicular to the one facing the light source,
- the ceiling, and
- a wall with its back to the light.

Therefore, under normal daylight conditions all surfaces of a room are articulated, even though they are all only one pigment color. Consider, for example, Color Art 7 which shows an all-white entryway with a chair and a console with topiaries in front of a staircase. The details of the entryway are articulated by light, shade, and shadow patterns and make a statement of quiet elegance and restraint.

Horizontal Surfaces

Because daylight enters the room from the sky above, the floor is usually the most brightly illuminated surface. The same color applied to wall, floor, and ceiling will appear lighter on the floor than on the other surfaces. If floor and ceiling colors are intended to match, the value of the floor color must be several shades darker.

A flat ceiling is illuminated indirectly by ambient light reflected from the floor and other surfaces but is brighter near an opening and darker farther away from it.

A slanted ceiling facing toward a window receives more light than a flat ceiling, and a slanted ceiling facing away from a window receives less light. A ceiling in which there is a skylight is darkest of all because of simultaneous contrast between the surface and the brightness of the sky.

Vertical Surfaces

The wall facing a window is the brightest vertical surface, and the darkest is the window wall with its back to the light. The same color applied to both walls appears appreciably darker on the window wall and lighter on the wall that receives illumination.

Glare is exacerbated where dark wall color is used on a window wall with its back to the light.

A reflector "light scoop" that reflects outside light onto a wall or ceiling can effectively increase its brightness (Moore, 1986, p. 40).

COLOR, TEXTURE, AND LIGHT REFLECTANCE

Whether a surface or an enclosure appears bright or dark depends on surface illumination and reflectance.

Shiny surfaces and high-value colors are highly reflective, whereas low-value colors and matte or rough finishes disperse the light. Dark colored, nonreflective surfaces appear dark, regardless of how well they are lighted.

Because of the adaptability of the eye, even a dimly lit room can seem bright. Brightness contrast created by value differences or by light, shade, and shadow patterns has greater impact than the actual amount of light in an interior.

9.2 VALUE SKETCH OF AN INTERIOR IN DAYLIGHT

a. Select an interior to sketch. White or one-color walls and a sunny day are preferred. Turn off all electric lights.

b. Make a value sketch using a soft pencil and a soft eraser on white sketch paper. Show value differences between patches of direct sunlight, shadows, and shade areas.

How do you distinguish between shadow and shade? What happens to the brightness of surfaces as they recede from the light source?

PERCENTAGE OF LIGHT REFLECTANCE

Both the light illuminating a surface and the light that it reflects can be measured with a light meter. The percentage of light that colors reflect is a measurement that enables you to judge their values for interior use. Some paint companies provide this information on each color chip.

The percentage of light reflectance of a color can also be ascertained by comparing it with a calibrated gray scale that provides this information for each value. Calibrated gray papers are included in the Color-aid color pack or may be purchased separately from the Color-aid Company (see the figure on page 63).

9.3 MEASURING THE FOOT-CANDLES OF DAYLIGHT RECEIVED BY INTERIOR SURFACES

a. Turn off all electric lights.
b. Measure with a light meter the amount of light falling on each surface by placing the bottom of the meter against the surface. Keep the face of the meter either vertical or face up so that the light strikes the light sensitive cell. Do not allow shadows to fall across the face of the meter.
c. Determine the average amount of light falling on the surface by taking readings at several places on the wall and averaging the results.

9.4 MEASURING THE FOOT-CANDLES OF DAYLIGHT REFLECTED BY AN INTERIOR SURFACE

a. Measure the amount of light reflected from the wall by placing the light sensitive cell of the light meter about 1 foot away from the wall.
b. Determine the average amount of light reflected by taking readings at several places on the surface, including areas that are directly lit, in shade, and in shadow, and averaging the results.

9.5 DETERMINING THE PERCENTAGE OF LIGHT REFLECTED BY A COLOR

a. Divide the average number of foot-candles a surface reflected by the average number of foot-candles received.
b. Compare the percentage of light reflected from a wall that you have measured with the percentage of light reflectance information from several color chips.

Would colors of the color chips appear darker, lighter, or the same as the color of the present wall?

RECOMMENDED SURFACE REFLECTANCE

The Illuminating Engineering Society of North America recommends the following light reflections for various locations and uses:

AREA	SURFACE	RANGE OF REFLECTANCE PERCENTAGES
General	Ceilings	70–90
	Walls	40–60
	Floors	0–50
Offices	Ceilings	80–90
	Partitions	40–70
	Walls	50–70
	Furniture	25–45
	Office equipment	25–45
	Floors	20–40
Residences	Ceilings	60–90
	Large curtains and draperies	35–60
	Walls	35–60
	Floors	15–35
Schools	Ceilings	70–90
	Walls	40–60
	Chalkboards	Up to 20
	Floors	30–50
Industry	Ceilings	80–90
	Walls	40–60
	Equipment and desk tops	25–45
	Floors	20+

SOURCE: IESNA, *Handbook,* 8th ed. 1993. Reprinted with permission.

Birren recommends that no color with a reflectance of less than 10 or 15 percent be used in a dimly lit interior, because colors very dark in value lose their identity in dim light. Above 25 to 30 foot-candles, the relationships between the steps of a value scale will remain normal (Birren, 1982, pp. 50–51).

HUE IN THE DAYLIT INTERIOR

ORIENTATION AND CLIMATE

The orientation of a room to the sun profoundly affects interior colors, for as the light varies, so does the color.

- North light is cool and steady with few shifting shadows, and is desired by artists for studios.
- South light is warm and constantly shifting, and it may need to be tempered during summer months.

- East light at sunrise is initially tinged with reddish orange, and progresses to neutral during the day.
- West light may be very warm and rich, particularly in the late afternoon (Faulkner, Nissen, and Faulkner, 1986, p. 408).

Change from a dominance of shorter to longer wavelengths can shift the light from bluish to reddish.

- The longer wavelengths in light enhance warm colors.
- The shorter wavelengths enhance cool colors.

The dominance of the longer reddish or shorter bluish wavelengths in daylight can vary with time of day, climate, and weather. Colors appear warmer and more highly saturated in bright light and subtly cooler and less saturated on a cloudy day, in a north light, in twilight, or in shade and shadow. Colors appear warmer and more highly saturated under tropical sunlight, at midday, or in a southern exposure; they appear softer and warmer in the light of a pink sunset. Colors appear cooler and softer under gray skies.

Light reflected from red clay and desert sand is warmer in color, whereas light reflected from a green landscape, a body of water, or a field of snow is cooler in color.

The quality of light entering a house or an interior complex can influence the way in which hues, values, and levels of saturation are distributed.

From a palette of coordinated hues, warm yellows, pinks, or orange tones could be used in rooms with a cold northern exposure. Less light from northern skies might suggest higher values and more saturated hues than would be called for in strong sunlight.

For rooms receiving hot afternoon sun, cool blue or green tones in higher values and softer tones could counter the perception of heat.

Depending on your point of view, dark colors might suggest either escape into the shade of a cool, woodsy retreat or refuge into a cozy den.

AMBIENT LIGHT AND HUE

Ambient light carries color from one surface to another. Recently, while sitting in an airplane, I thought either that colored lights had been used to illuminate a section of the plane in front of me or that the surface had been painted pink. Then I discovered that the pinkness was caused by red reflected from a woman's dress.

As colors reflect into each other, each interior color surface assumes attributes of the surface facing it. For example:

- A green wall opposite another green wall will be more intensely green than if it were opposite a white wall.
- A white wall opposite a green wall will pick up greenness.
- A blue wall opposite a yellow wall will appear greenish blue, and the yellow wall will tend toward greenish yellow.
- Light reflected from a red carpet will tint a white ceiling pink.

Although ambient color may be used to advantage, it contributes in no small way to the difficulty of predicting how a color will appear in an interior.

THE TEMPERATURE OF LIGHT

PHYSICAL TEMPERATURE

The physical temperature of light is the opposite of its perceived temperature:

- The higher the physical temperature of light, the bluer or colder it appears.
- The lower the physical temperature, the redder or yellower or warmer it appears.

The physical temperature of light is based on the principle of black-body radiation. When an iron bar is slowly heated, its color changes from black to invisible infrared, to dull red, then orange, yellow, blue, and at its highest temperature it becomes white hot (Gardner and Hannaford, 1993, p. 5).

The physical temperature of light is measured in degrees kelvin (K). At 2000 K candlelight is the coolest of all the light sources, yet it casts a warm, cozy light, whereas bluish light from the northern sky at 8000 K or more is perceived as cold.

- Below 3300 K light is perceived as warm.
- From 3300 to 5300 K light is perceived as intermediate.
- Above 5300 K light is perceived as cold.

The color of summer midday sun lies roughly in the middle of the range between candlelight and a clear blue northern sky (Gardner and Hannaford, 1993, p. 5).

COLOR-RENDERING CAPABILITIES OF LIGHT SOURCES

Each electric light source commonly used for interior illumination:

- approximates sunlight, in that each spectrum falls within the violet-to-red range; and
- differs from sunlight, in that some are biased toward the longer wavelengths and others are biased toward the shorter wavelengths.

The color rendering capability of a light source is determined by how it makes colors appear in comparison with the way they appear in daylight (Color Art 56*A*). Color quality is judged to be good to the extent that colors are not distorted beyond what perceptual constancy can accept.

Light sources most commonly used for general lighting in interiors are *tungsten incandescent*, *tungsten halogen*, and *fluorescent*. Because of their versatility, these light sources have been developed into a vast array of forms to meet a vast array of lighting requirements.

Tungsten Filament

Tungsten filament lamps at 3000 K or less are the most widely used form of incandescent lighting. The light they emit emphasizes warm reds and oranges and suppresses blues and greens (Color Art 56*B*). Because of its warmth incandescent light flatters the human complexion and can create an atmosphere of intimacy. It is widely favored for general lighting in homes and places where people gather, and in low wattage it can simulate candlelight (Gardner and Hannaford, 1993, p. 16). It is widely used in bars or restaurants where low levels of lighting are desired.

Tungsten Halogen

The tungsten halogen lamp is a refinement of the incandescent tungsten lamp. With a color temperature at above 3000 K, tungsten halogen lamps are generally considered to offer a better quality of light, or light closer to daylight, than their incandescent counterparts. They offer good color rendering, making colors appear crisp and sharp. They are widely used in retailing because they give brightness and sparkle to merchandise and interiors (Gardner and Hannaford, 1993, pp. 17 and 19) (Color Art 56C).

Fluorescent

Although its color rendering has been improved dramatically since it first appeared, the perceived effect of fluorescent lighting is "at best flat and bland and at worst cold and unfriendly"—never quite as good as daylight or equivalent incandescent sources (Color Art 56*D*). The addition of other types of lamps can create highlighting and make the interior more interesting (Gardner and Hannaford, 1993, pp. 21–22) (Color Art 56*E*).

Whether a fluorescent light is cool or warm or whether its color rendering is excellent or poor depends on the exact mix of phosphor powders coating the inside of the tube, which are manufacturers' trade secrets. There are many different versions of "warm white" and "cool white" fluorescent tubes on the market, but these can vary widely in their color rendering capabilities (Gardner and Hannaford, 1993, p. 22).

WHAT IS "NORMAL" ILLUMINATION?

Light in the interior appears normal:

- under high levels of cool light, such as fluorescent or halogen light, and
- under low levels of warm light, such as candlelight or firelight (Birren, 1982, p. 36).

These correspond to the cold, bright light at midday and the warm glow of sunset. The world does not appear normal under high levels of warm light or low levels of cold light.

> *Luckily people still have enough romantic feeling not to want to throw out every light source which does not resemble daylight. We still love to sit by the wood fire in our fireplaces, or sing and dance around the camp fire. Candlelight makes our dinner more intimate and full of atmosphere. We also choose lamplight instead of "daylight imitating" lights for our ordinary living quarters.* (Gerritsen, 1983, pp. 31–32)

> *A cocktail lounge would suggest live ghouls and dead ghosts if it were illuminated by dim blue or violet light, whereas a school classroom or office under brilliant red or pink light would be visually and psychologically objectionable.* (Birren, 1982, p. 37)

CONSTANCY AND ADAPTATION

Although the amount of light falling on a surface and reflected from it can be measured, the appearance of objects and surfaces under various light conditions cannot. This is because of constancy and adaptation.

White appears white whether seen in less than a fraction of a foot-candle or under hundreds of foot-candles of light (Birren, 1982, p. 42) or under warm or cool light. In a room painted white some areas directly lit may be excessively bright and other areas in shade or shadow may appear almost black, but the room will still be perceived as white. The brain makes the necessary comparisons, computes the nature of the differences, and decides that the color is continuous. Were it not so, patches of lights and darks and edges could break up the visual field into unrelated bits and pieces, producing chaos and confusion and disrupting form constancy.

Color constancy allows colors to be recognized regardless of the time of day, distance, or change in position. A green surface appears green under a wide variety of light sources ranging from warm to cool and from bright to dim. One color used on all surfaces of an interior appears to be the same color throughout despite differences in the illumination.

Form stabilizes the expected colors of things despite wide color variations. Apples are apples whether the artist paints them pink or purple, and we have little difficulty with a painting that shows grass not only green but orange and magenta as well (Livingstone, 1988, p. 81).

The differences between warm and cool illumination are best perceived when observed from outside the room:

> *Sitting in an office under incandescent light, another office across the street or court illuminated by fluorescent light will appear bluish. Or in the reverse situation, the incandescent-lit office will look yellowish to anyone sitting in a fluorescent-lit room.* (Birren, 1982, p. 42)

When colors are viewed within an interior under one type of light, either warm or cool, the warmth or coolness is not apparent. As your eye adapts to the light source, you see the world as normal, even though the light may be warmer or cooler than daylight or even colored.

Even though the colors appear normal, the pervasive blueness of a cool incandescent light or a warm fluorescent light influences the visual temperature and affects both hue and saturation (Birren, 1982, p. 42).

9.6 THE EFFECTS OF DIFFERENT LIGHT SOURCES ON COLORS

A box divided into two compartments, each fitted with incandescent, halogen, and warm and cool fluorescent lamps, provides a way to compare the effects of the various light spectra on colors. The box should be large enough so that identical models with the same colors in both can be viewed in the two compartments at the same time under different light conditions.

METAMERISM

Because colors appear different under different types of illumination,

- the lighting should be in place before the colors are selected, and
- colors should be tested under the illumination in which they are to be seen.

In Chapter 8, we saw that one color can appear to be two different colors under two different kinds of illumination. It is equally true that two colors, with different hue ingredients in their intermixes, may appear to be the same color under two different lights.

The spectra of daylight, incandescent, tungsten halogen, and warm and cool fluorescent lights all differ as to their dominant wavelengths. Blue will be enhanced by a cool fluorescent light, but will appear dingy under a warmer incandescent light. A dominantly warm light will enhance the redness in magenta, but a dominantly cool light will emphasize its blueness.

Matching colors under different light sources is a problem, not only for the building and furnishings industries but for anyone who needs to match colors of different materials.

PERCEIVED ROOM TEMPERATURE

Although the physical temperature of a room can be measured with a thermometer, the perception of warmth or coolness cannot. Color in light, surface color, and the textures of materials are all interrelated in the perception of room temperature, quite apart from the physical temperature of a room.

Although some warmth seems to be essential in order to "humanize" architecture, people vary in their preferences for warmth or coolness.

HUE, LIGHT, AND THE PERCEPTION OF WARMTH OR COOLNESS

The perception of the warmth or coolness of colors is reinforced by their relationship to perceived room temperature. Itten tells of experiments that demonstrated that people felt colder in a workroom painted blue-green and warmer in one painted red-orange. In the blue–green room the occupants felt cold when the temperature was 59°F, but they did not feel cold in the red-orange room until the temperature fell between 52 and 54°F (Itten, 1970, p. 45).

Similarly, you are more likely to feel chilly under a cool fluorescent light and warmer under a warm incandescent light. This has more to do with the appearance of the light than with the fact that fluorescent light emits less heat than does incandescent.

MATERIALS AND SURFACE TEMPERATURE

The architectural interior is also a tactile environment. Because of the warmth of fabric upholstery and curtains, floor coverings, and wood furniture, these have long been recognized as primary transition elements that relate people to buildings and make architecture habitable. Upholstery fabrics are especially important because they come in direct contact with the body. In a cold climate materials cold to the touch exacerbate the sense of coldness of an interior, even though the heating system works, the light is incandescent, and the colors are warm. Warm materials are preferred, because they lend a sense of warmth to an interior. In hot climates rattan, cotton, and other cool-to-the-touch materials are widely used.

Architectural materials—stone, brick, ceramic tile, glass, metal, and the like—are not only cold to the touch, they absorb heat from the room. Touch them and you can experience their surface temperatures directly. Aside from their artistic merit, tapestries in medieval castles not only kept out the cold, but provided tactile warmth as well.

Animal products are warmest to the touch, with fur warmest of all. Wool and silk are warmer to the touch than cotton, and leather is warmer than vinyl. Organic plant materials, such as wood, paper, cotton, or linen, are cooler to the touch than animal products but warmer than synthetics, and synthetics are warmer than stone, glass, or metal. The popularity of wood is due in large part to the warmth of its surface temperature.

Materials are experienced by the eye as well as by the sense of touch. You know that fur is soft and that glass is hard and smooth by the way that they appear. A rich wall covering is not to be handled, but it can impart warmth and elegance to a room by the way it appears. Embossing and gilt make the wall covering in Color Art 57 extremely rich and reflective, imparting warmth, luxury, and formal elegance to an interior.

9.7 PERCEIVED TEMPERATURE OF THE ROOM YOU ARE IN

Do you judge the room where you are to be warm or cool? What is the temperature? Touch the materials in the room around you. Which are warm and which are cool to the touch? Are the colors of the room dominantly warm or cool? Is the interior lighting dominantly warm or cool? What is the temperature outside? What are the light conditions outside? What effect does the quality of daylight have on the sense of warmth or coolness inside?

TYPES OF LIGHT SOURCES

POINT AND DISPERSED LIGHT SOURCES

A point source of light emanates light outward in all directions from the center, casting light, shadow, and shade patterns that are quite different from those cast by the parallel rays of sunlight. A point source can either provide diffuse light or be focused as a spot that creates pools of bright light.

Multiple point sources can create overlapping pools of light or cast multiple overlapping shadows on surfaces. Focused point sources can create shadows that highlight architectural details and the sculptural forms of objects (Color Art 58).

Ceiling fluorescent fixtures create luminous ceilings of dispersed light that cast no shadows. Indirect light sources disperse light by directing it onto the ceiling or other surfaces to be reflected into the room as ambient light.

9.8 VALUE SKETCH OF AN INTERIOR SHOWING EFFECTS OF MULTIPLE LIGHT SOURCES

a. Make a value sketch of an interior that is lit by multiple light sources.
b. Note overlapping pools of light and multiple shadows. Note the effects of shadowless light.

How do light, shadow, and shade in this sketch differ from that in Exercise 9.2?

GRAZING AND WALL WASHING

When light is directed onto a wall or ceiling, the surface itself is not only brightened, but reflected light illuminates the room and is distributed throughout an interior. The ambient light becomes a secondary light source. Light can be focused on a wall so that it flows over the surface.

- *Grazing* is achieved by placing lighting fixtures on the ceiling or on the floor close to the wall.
- *Wall washing* is achieved by placing the lighting fixtures on the ceiling or floor about 3 feet out from the wall, so that the wall has uniform brightness from top to bottom.

Grazing emphasizes natural textures and sculptural relief of the surface, but it can also show up imperfections. Wall washing heightens color and textural shadows, but small imperfections do not show (Gordon and Nuckolls, 1995, p. 31).

COLORED LIGHT

INTERIOR SURFACES

Under colored light:

- A surface hue is intensified if illuminated by corresponding light wavelengths.
- A surface hue will appear black if illuminated by a light of its complementary hue.
- A surface hue can be influenced toward the color of the light if the light is an adjacent hue.

Because colored light differs so drastically from daylight, it is not used for general illumination in the living environment. It does strange things to the human complexion and distorts the symbolic meanings of familiar things in the environment. Red light renders green plants black, blue and violet lights bring out unflattering blue skin tones that make you appear ill, and food under colored light can be rendered unpalatable.

However, for special design effects, grazing or washing colored light on a wall surface is potentially a rich source of color. The use of colored light in the living or work space must be dealt with judiciously. One wall lit with brilliant color could be an accent, but if all interior surfaces were bathed in colored light, the volume of space would appear hued and the people could appear strangely colored.

In Robert Irwin's lighted space, "Radial," in the Musée d'Arte Moderne de la Ville de Paris, 1994 (Color Art 59), the space itself appears orange-yellow.

COLD CATHODE TUBING

The neon light so familiar in advertising is an example of cold cathode lighting. Neon tubes can be obtained in any color and bent into any shape. Neon light has challenged artists to create sculptural and graphic designs suitable for interior use as well as for commercial applications.

TEXTURE AND LIGHT REFLECTANCE

The texture of a material has as much to do with its color quality as a violin, a harp, or a xylophone has to do with the quality of a musical tone. How a material absorbs and reflects light, casts shadows upon itself, or filters the light affects its colors and luminosity and reveals the characteristics of the material.

Materials are sensed by both touch and sight. The textures and colors of materials humanize interior space and establish its general ambience, and are also important bearers of meaning.

In the lobby of a bank's corporate headquarters (Color Art 28), light woods, cream-colored lacquered panels, rich fabrics, and marble floors are unifying elements that continue throughout, serving as background for artwork, deep blues, and other rich colors.

ARCHITECTURAL SURFACES

Texture and Surface Articulation

A smooth finish reveals the gradation of light, shade, and shadow on an architectural surface more effectively than a roughly-textured surface that disperses the light. Imperfections on a wall surface can be camouflaged by rough texture, but are exaggerated by a smooth, shiny treatment.

Matte or rough finishes tend to camouflage edges and minimize the directional differences of planes. The form of an object with a smooth, shiny finish will be clearly articulated, but with a matte finish it may appear as a flat surface. A curved wall with a rough surface could appear flat (Nayar and Oren, 1995, pp.1153–1155).

Wall Finishes

Most painted walls and wallpapers are given a matte finish that disperses light and softens color. As you saw in Chapter 8, the luminosity of a color is increased as transparent colorants or finishes permit the light to penetrate the surface and to be reflected back and forth through the surface.

Highly reflective glossy enamels and metallic finishes tend to lighten and intensify colors but can create glare (Color Art 60). High gloss dark or vivid wall colors can sometimes appear gaudy and unpleasant, even though black, shiny floors may seem sophisticated.

Highlighting enhances embossed and textured materials, revealing surface design through subtle light, shade, and shadow patterns. The coarse textures of grass cloth, burlap, and similar materials derive their three-dimensional character from the shadows that the texture casts on the surface. Simulated textures with shadow effects painted into the design and designs that create convincing illusions of molding can give the appearance of surface depth, but they reflect light like the flat surfaces that they are.

The means of creating textural effects on wall coverings are apparently inexhaustible—flocking, satin finishes, iridescent paints, metallic paints, glitter, and so on.

INTERIOR MATERIALS

Fabrics

The light reflectance of a fabric texture is determined by its fiber, yarn twist, weave, and finish. It can be napped, pile, smooth and shiny, or matte. It can be of a tight or loose weave; it can be transparent, translucent, or opaque; it can reflect or filter light, or both. It can drape in soft folds or lend itself to crisp pleats.

The grain of velvet or a pile weave carpet is determined by the direction of its pile, which appears shinier and lighter in color when lighted with the grain but darker and richer when lighted against the grain (Color Art 61). Its richness and depth are due to the shadows that individual tufts cast on other tufts. Black velvet could well be the blackest of all blacks.

Velvet and satin dyed in the same vat will differ drastically in value because they reflect light differently. The smooth fibers and long floating threads of satin give it its characteristic highly reflective, luxurious sheen. The pattern of a one-color damask is apparent because its long floating warp and weft threads reflect light differently.

Like satin, sateen also has floating threads that give it a glossy surface, but its cotton fibers are less reflective than those of silk or nylon. Chintz also has sheen, but this is due to its tight plain weave and finish. Calendering is a finish that gives both chintz and sateen a shiny surface and a characteristic crispness. When illuminated from behind, their colors become brilliant in the same way as does stained glass.

Nubby, loosely twisted yarns also disperse light on a fabric, whereas smooth yarns give it a shinier appearance. Tightly twisted yarns give crepe a matte finish.

A loose weave permits light to penetrate a curtain. A sheer curtain filters and softens the light entering an interior, and if it is tinted, it seems to color the light coming through it.

The folds of a curtain illuminated obliquely will have directly lit, shade, and shadow areas that emphasize both the drapability of the fabric and its inherent textural characteristics. Pleats are emphasized in the same way.

Wood

Wood is generally a complex warm neutral color that reflects all spectral hues. Orange or yellow is usually the dominant hue, although in mahogany red is prominent and in walnut purple may be discernible.

A polished wood is more luminous than an unpolished wood. An unpolished wood reflects light directly off its outer surface, whereas the deeper color of wood with a clear finish is the result of multiple reflections. Not all of the light that penetrates the finish is reflected outward, some of it being returned to the bottom surface, where selective absorption takes place a second time or more (Beck, 1972, p. 153), giving wood great depth and richness.

Metal

The glint of light reflected from highly polished metals, such as a brass door knob or a silver urn, provides a jewel-like accent to an interior. Metals can be given a variety of finishes, such as burnished brass or weathered copper.

Gold metal appears yellow, silver appears gray, and copper a reddish brown in color, but polished metals cannot be replicated in paint, because they reflect all of the light that falls on them (Kuehni, 1983, p. 42).

Crystal and Glass

Glass can be clear, translucent, or opaque; it can be colored, textured, or smooth, and it can assume any shape. It can transmit, reflect, and refract light.

Probably no other material can generate a degree of excitement comparable to a cut crystal chandelier in candlelight with hundreds of prisms sparkling like diamonds. Crystal and glass are also jewels in an interior.

A mirror reflects all of the light that falls on it, the reflected image including any glitter that happens to be present.

The thicker a glass table top is, the more complex are its effects on light. Some light is reflected from the surface, some light is reflected back and forth within the thickness of the glass, some light is refracted—perhaps picking up color—and some light passes through the glass as though it were a lens.

Ultimately, materials and furnishings are transition materials and objects necessary to humanize architecture and make it habitable.

10 THE PERSONAL AND PUBLIC IMAGE OF INTERIOR COLOR

Although we all share the same type of visual apparatus, we do not all see the same colors in the same way. This is because we have all had different visual experiences in our backgrounds.

Your *mental image* of interior color is derived from all of your cumulative experiences with interior color and the symbolic meanings associated with them. This provides you with a basis for comparing and judging incoming information from interiors and interior colors and for forming opinions regarding their meanings. *The broader your background of experience with seeing and using interior color, the better equipped you are to make color judgments.*

As enough people within a society come to share a common image of interior color, a trend develops. Color trends express the public mood and come and go with more or less predictable regularity.

SYMBOLS AND MENTAL IMAGES

Your cumulative background of visual experiences determines what you see and understand. Boulding calls this background the *image.* Your mental image of interior color is a composite of all of your lifetime experiences seeing, learning about, and using interior color.

The brain has the amazing ability to transform the jumble of visual stimuli falling on the retina into *symbolic meanings* (Langer, 1951, p. 46).

- Symbols are *what the brain thinks with.*
- Symbolic meanings are *what you see.*

Symbolic meanings of interior color—what it "says"—are far stronger than its dynamic qualities—what it "does"—and until you acquire color information, you probably think of color in terms of whether or not it is appropriate or whether or not you like it.

SYMBOLIC MEANINGS OF COLOR

A symbol stands for something beyond itself. Red, white, and blue—the colors of the flag—are symbols of the United States, and patriots declare their patriotism by waving the flag. Orange and purple are the school colors, red and green symbolize Christmas, and black and orange stand for Halloween. Blue is your favorite color—blue "looks like you"; it reminds you of something enjoyed and makes you feel happy; your blue bedroom is a symbol of you. Ducks and chickens on the wallpaper might be deemed appropriate symbols for a child's room but inappropriate for a living room or an office.

High-saturation colors may be considered advancing, exciting, loud, or clashing; low-saturation colors may be considered receding, soft, bland, serene, or quiet. These are meanings *attributed* to colors by your brain based on your previous visual experiences. The brain compares colors that you see against this color image in your mind and draws a conclusion as to what they mean. The color itself is only reflected wavelengths, totally inert, with no intent whatsoever; *color has no mind of its own and has meaning only because you read meaning into it.*

Warm or cool, hot or cold, loud or soft, strident or serene, bland or exciting, clashing or blending—these are symbolic color meanings in themselves, but the symbolic response does not stop there. Remember that color is never seen in the abstract but always as colored something, and that color judgments are never made in a vacuum. You attribute symbolic meanings to colors in the context of their associations with people, places, functional uses, feelings, and so on. A red rose says "I love you," but it is also a metaphor for unrequited love, as in the old song, "... but my false lover pulled the rose, but, aye, he left the thorn wi' me."

Deciphering the tacit meanings of interior color is comparable to "reading between the lines" of the newspaper in order to grasp the more obscure implications of what is being said. Many nuances of meaning are conveyed if the observer has the sensitivity and the background of experience to become aware of them.

SIGNS VERSUS SYMBOLS

The difference between signs and symbols is that signs are more direct. A green light says "go," the arrow says "go that way," the blue door says "enter here." To the cat the sound of a refrigerator door opening is a sign of food. Signs as such stand for little beyond their present function, although deeper meanings can be attributed to them. A red light can symbolize frustration; the go-ahead green light can be interpreted as a symbol of the pathway to success without obstruction.

SYMBOLS AND CULTURE

Color meanings are culture based, and some symbols can be understood only if you are familiar with the culture or the tradition. According to one story, an onlooker remarked to Picasso that she did not understand modern art. When he asked her if she understood Chinese, she replied that she did not. His response was that 500,000,000 people do. You have to know the code. Unless you know Japanese, you cannot read Japanese calligraphy, but you can admire its grace and beauty. Hanging on your wall, it is a sign of your excellent taste. If you come from a society in which black is associated with death, you might not suspect that in China white symbolizes death and is used at funerals.

THE MENTAL IMAGE AS A VALUE SYSTEM

The term "image", as defined by Boulding, refers *to your own subjective knowledge of the world—what you believe to be true* (emphasis added) (Boulding, 1966, p. 6).

Boulding reminds us that "there are no such things as 'facts.' There are only messages filtered through a changeable value system" (Boulding, 1966, p. 14). Your mental image of interior color determines not only what you see but how you interpret it, assess its merits, and feel about it.

Some symbols are elusive, at least in part, because different people read different meanings into what they see. If you believe that orange and green "fight," that is the way you will see them, but if you believe that they blend beautifully, you will see them as an agreeable combination.

THE INFLUENCE OF KNOWLEDGE

What you know about interior color determines what you believe to be true. Your understanding of how it is perceived, its dynamic and expressive qualities, how to create and use it determines how you see interior color and judge its merits.

Knowledge of the historic uses of interior color and familiarity with trendy colors and colors that well-known designers use—these influence your mental image of color.

So does your understanding of color science and technology. If you believe in the fundamental system of hue organization as fundamental truth, you will see and use color one way, but if you believe that truth lies in a color system based on spectral and basic hues, you will approach color somewhat differently.

As your knowledge of color and exposure to color uses expands, your mental image of interior color changes.

COLOR IN THE INTERIOR

Within an instant after you walk into a room, you may have already checked its color against your mental image of interior color, and made a judgment as to its appropriateness, how you feel about it, and what it reminds you of. The mental image you hold of interior color determines the meanings you read into colors, things, and places, and provides the criteria against which you judge which colors are appropriate for various settings. If you lack color awareness, however, you might not even notice color.

Whether you like or dislike a color is often based on pleasant or unpleasant associations. Lavender reminds you of great aunt Martha; it, therefore, stands as a symbol of her. If great aunt Martha is a warm, wonderful person, lavender might be your favorite color, but if she is a grouchy, unpleasant soul, you might dislike it intensely.

Your personal image of interior color is unique to yourself alone. There can be as many assessments of a given interior as there are people doing the assessing. People with similar backgrounds of experience and training are more likely to agree on whether a given color is "good" or appropriate for a particular setting than people with different backgrounds.

I might consider a high saturation color in a person's living room to be loud, vulgar and gaudy, and consider the person who owns it "brassy" and having poor taste. I might make disparaging inferences about that person's social class, education, taste, sensitivity to the environment, personality traits, and so on. You, however, coming from a different background, might consider both the color and the person happy, exuberant, uninhibited, carefree, and exciting. Even though neither of us might intellectualize our reactions or use these particular words, we would respond in terms of feelings evoked, perhaps by simply liking or disliking the color or the person.

As the color image goes, so goes the opinion.

WALLPAPER AND MEANINGS

The design community often appears to be divided into two camps—those who like wallpaper and those who hate it. The general public, however, likes wallpaper.

The major problem with wallpaper in the judgment of many designers lies with the meanings conveyed, which far outweigh any dynamic effects. Despite the availability of "good" wallpapers, many or even most patterns are seen by the discriminating eye as hackneyed, the colors bland and innocuous, and the message one of weak sentimentality or cuteness. Some patterns may be ostentatious or overpowering or may not express a particular lifestyle as desired. Yet some patterns can bring richness to an interior far beyond what flat color can provide. I recall a woman's bedroom in which a blue floral wallpaper covered walls and ceilings, and the bedspread and tester were the same color and pattern. It was charming and unforgettable. Elegant wall pattern can make an elegant interior more elegant, and a casual, carefree pattern can reinforce the meanings conveyed by casual furnishings and lifestyle.

Wallpaper or any other decorative use of pattern, such as upholstery or curtain fabrics, makes an extremely individual statement and should be chosen with discrimination. Appropriateness is an instinctive judgment that must be made according to the context.

DESIGN PROFESSIONALS AND THE IMAGE OF INTERIOR COLOR

Architects and interior designers have not always agreed on matters of interior color and pattern or, for that matter, on a number of design concerns. Because of their disparate histories, each of the two professions has had its own image of what constitutes good design.

Architecture, with its roots in beaux arts and Bauhaus, developed an intellectual regard for form and function. Modern architects have shown a preference for crisp, uncluttered white and primary colors or the colors of natural materials, such as wood, stone, marble, and foliage.

Interior design, with its roots in the antiques trade, decorating, and retailing, had its finger on the pulse of "what the public wants"—and what the public wanted was the sensuous appeal of touch, warmth, enclosure, and the opportunity to indulge its unabashed love of accumulating artifacts.

Within the last half century, differences between the two professional images of interiors have been mitigated—note the term "interior architecture." Interior design has been influenced by the discipline imposed by form and function and by awareness of the interior environment as a social, psychological, and behavioral setting. Architecture has recognized that an empty building is unlivable and that the colors and objects that people like personalize a building, relate it to human experience, and make it habitable.

Differing images still separate design professionals with regard to interior color, and you may judge for yourself which currents of thought and feeling influence your own attitudes toward design.

THE BEIGE, GRAY, AND OFF-WHITE SYNDROME

If people's mental image of interiors does not include color, wonderful color in particular, it can mean little or nothing to them. They simply do not see it because they have nothing to see it with. On finding an unusual use of lavender in a hospital corridor, I asked the receptionist how she liked the color. Her reply was that she had not noticed it and had no opinion about it.

Lack of awareness or fear of hue is manifest in a world of beige, gray, or off-white interior environments—offices, homes, hospitals, day-care centers, restaurants, shops—everywhere you look. Warm neutrals can make exceptionally satisfying backgrounds and are most often the color of choice. Although neutrals can be rich, complex intermixes, most often they are not and are simply preferred because they are safe.

When asked to make interior color choices, some people may select gray or beige or off-white because that is the extent of their color vocabulary. This preference for neutrals is also shared by designers and architects, either because they believe that is what their clients want, or because they think that hue is not needed or might detract from the structure, or quite possibly because they are not sure of their ability to use color. People who live in a world without hue are immune to the excitement and delight of wonderful color and to the way it can enliven the outlook, raise the spirit, and put people in touch with their surroundings.

Some people fear that they will tire of a color or that it will convey the wrong message, be overly stimulating or depressing, or not "go" with other colors. It has been said that divorces have been caused by brown wallpaper. People can become so inured to offensive or innocuous color that they cease to see it, and by "tuning it out" they become insensitive to their environment. Insensitivity, however, does not make depressing color any less depressing.

Clients' lack of interior color awareness makes them reluctant to undertake color decisions, and they are vulnerable to whatever an "expert" tells them. It behooves the expert, therefore, to have real color expertise and the personal freedom to use it.

The designer's goal is to create environment colors that lift the spirit. *The challenge is not the crashing discord but the safe and ordinary, the practical*—the beige, gray, and off-white syndrome.

TRADITION AND THE TYRANNY OF THE SYMBOL

Tradition is a link with historical roots, whether inherited or adopted or sought. Any tradition from any part of the world and from whatever century provides its own unique vocabulary of design forms and color uses that are recognized by those who espouse it.

Despite the considerable scope and flexibility of the symbols within it, a tradition is basically a system of "right answers" that inhibits experimentation beyond its boundaries. Knowing that one has a "right answer" or a "right color" is comforting to those who seek the acceptance of those versed in the tradition. Style and status, however, are more likely to be symbolized by the structure, the forms of furnishings, and the textures of materials than by color. Any environment color can be used practically anywhere. In this regard color is the more democratic element.

To one steeped in 18th-century English or "country" traditions, "modern" furnishings do not convey the desired meanings and seem cold and barren. Eighteenth century English furnishings, which may appear to some as an anomaly in a steel and glass skyscraper office, may be chosen by the traditionalist because they are considered a warmer and more human transition between people and building or are recognized as a familiar prestige symbol.

Yet there remains the innate human need for "the variable, the contrasting, and the least expected" (Fiske and Maddi, 1961, p. 409)—the excitement of the new that cannot be met by that which is safe and familiar, regardless of how beautiful it may be. To step outside a tradition and try new ideas requires openness of mind, independent thinking, and willingness to take risk. Oberascher states:

> *It is to be expected that people with traditional attitudes adhere to a more "traditional color world" than those with more liberal and unconventional attitudes....*
> *Therefore, willingness to adapt new ideas seems to be a prerequisite for the acceptance of a new color range.* (Oberascher in Linton, 1994, p. 76)

Design symbols are so powerful that they can obscure other aspects of the design challenge. People can be more concerned with the appropriateness of style, whether traditional or avant garde, than with function or the dynamics of color, light, form, and space. Considerable intellectual effort is required to see beyond symbolic meanings to other aspects of design and design theory, such as are discussed in this book.

You need to be aware of the power of the symbol, to be able to see through and beyond it, and to be able to use and control it rather than being subservient to it.

SOME INTERIOR COLOR MEANINGS

HOMES

An interior stands as a powerful symbol of the people who inhabit the space. The colors and furnishings that personalize homes and rooms convey much information about the lifestyles and aspirations of the occupants, their social and cultural backgrounds, their individual personalities, ages, eccentricities, the values they hold, and how they regard the interior environment.

The living room, in particular, often establishes the standing of the family within its peer group by being similar enough to the living rooms of others to be acceptable, yet different enough to express individuality. Interior color is often carefully chosen to convey just exactly the "right" nuance of meaning. People have had nervous breakdowns trying to get a "right" color.

PEOPLE

Women and Men

Many age-old stereotypes regarding women and men have become obsolete. Women as well as men are often breadwinners, and women of all ages are active participants in every aspect of business, political, and professional life. Grandmothers are no longer considered candidates for lavender and old lace and rocking chairs. Men are no longer considered to be incapable of caring for home and children.

When a woman stayed home to raise a family and manage the house, the house was her domain, often characterized by the dominance of tints—the supposedly "feminine" colors. Weak tints, somehow out of character with the masculine temperament, implied that the men and boys of the house were out of place in their own home. Deeper, more positive colors seem more symbolic of masculinity as well as of the changing roles of women.

Today colors and patterns throughout the house are more likely to express the identity of all members of the family. Color in individual rooms, however, often establishes the territory of particular members of the family.

Children

Pale tints of pink and blue have long been a metaphor for the fragility of the newborn, but today's healthy babies do not seem to stay so fragile for very long. Stronger primary colors prevail in clothing, toys, and furnishings for tots, symbolizing their energy and activity and arousing their interest. These colors are in keeping with the more robust health of young children, when compared with babies in former generations.

Efforts to personalize the rooms of young children sometimes lead to wallpaper. Little boys are supposed to like ships or horses or dogs, and little girls are supposed to like dolls or pink ruffles, so realistic representations of such are often used as motifs. All too often the design is trite and unimaginative and has little to do with the surface (Chapter 4), so that the child is taught poor design from an early age. Instead, well-designed wallpaper or solid colors could provide an interesting background for cherished artifacts, and toys rather than pictures on the wallpaper could stimulate the imagination.

PUBLIC OR BUSINESS INTERIORS

What are "good" colors for public places? Do they differ from colors for the home and, if so, how? Are colors for anonymous groups different from colors that are uniquely individual?

Colors and furnishings that humanize private places are often used to humanize public places—without them business settings, churches, and schools could be sterile territories. If a medical facility or a bank interior appears too "cute" or personal or eccentric, however, you might be made to feel as though you were intruding into private territory.

The following vignettes describe interiors with symbolic connotations:

- The reception room of an academic building was to be repainted in its original soft rose color. When the new paint was on the walls, however, it became evident that the color was just slightly more saturated than before, and the effects were devastating—the color was compared to that of a bordello, no less! The reception room was again repainted, this time in a softer tone.
- Floral chintz ruffles and bric-a-brac are intended to make a cafeteria appear "homey," but with no apparent awareness of the relationship between the

furnishings, the background color, and the space. The decor appeals to the unsophisticated clientele, but to others it appears cluttered and colorless, and the artifacts intended to evoke nostalgia appear naive.

- Patrons of a hotel dining room were greeted with soft rose color—elegant and dignified, understated, and expensive. Pink tablecloths, pink candles, fresh flowers, gleaming crystal, polished silver, and dim lighting exuded romantic elegance.
- Marble floors, thick carpets, and steel trim conveyed a sense of crisp efficiency, calm restraint, dignity, and financial power for the corporate offices of a steel manufacturer. Gray was the dominant color, chosen because it symbolized the product and echoed the corporate image—light gray for walls and dark gray upholstery on metal furniture. Accents of white and colorful abstract impressionist paintings enlivened the scene.
- The polished wood of the basketball court was a warm, yellowish neutral background against which the players moved. The walls and ceiling of the structure, however, had been treated with an orange wood stain—a harsh, unpleasant color that could be disturbing to the critical eye. Fortunately, the attention was riveted on the game, and few paid much attention to the colors of the surround.
- The interior of St. Luke's Church needed painting. Its off-white color was deemed too sterile, so the walls were painted light green. No sooner was the color on the walls than the congregation agreed that it was the wrong color—too bedroomy. The church was repainted off-white and the congregation was happy.
- Individual rooms in the retirement home opened onto a tunnel-like corridor that extended the entire length of the long building, with windows located at both ends. Light at the end of a long corridor is said to symbolize death.

10.1 ANALYSIS OF THE SYMBOLIC MEANINGS CONVEYED BY PHOTOGRAPHS OF HOME INTERIORS

Find two photographs of home interiors in magazines or photograph two home interiors. (Interiors you photograph should be anonymous.) Compare the two as to what they reveal about the occupants—how they are alike and how they differ.

What inferences can you draw about the people who inhabit the space?

Is the space occupied by a single person, a family, or other social group?

Is this a space for a man, woman, or child? What are their ages? Interests? Activities?

What is their educational level? Income bracket? Social status?

To what peer group do they belong? To what peer group do they belong or aspire? What do they consider important?

What can you tell about their taste? Their awareness of their surroundings?

What key symbols convey this information—the structure, the furniture, the artifacts, the textures of materials or finishes, the patterns, the colors?

10.2 ANALYSIS OF THE SYMBOLIC MEANINGS CONVEYED BY PHOTOGRAPHS OF OFFICES

Find or take two photographs of office interiors. Compare them as to what they tell you about the occupants—how they are alike and how they differ.

What inferences can you draw about the people who inhabit the space? What type of company is it? What services or products does it provide?
Where is it located? What difference does the location make?
Who uses the space—the chief executive officer, the receptionist, the secretary, or other?
How large or small is the company? How modest or powerful?
What image does it present to the public?

What key symbols convey this information—the structure, the furniture, the artifacts, the textures of materials or finishes, the patterns, the colors?

NAMES OF INTERIOR COLORS

People who name interior colors, like people who name streets or real estate developments, search for words that conjure up romantic images or nostalgia for the past, the simple life, ancestors, the exotic, or the prestigious. Such symbols sell both paint and real estate, although they have nothing to do with the product itself.

The story was told by a paint company representative that the color "Ivory" became passé and sales went down, but when the name was changed to "Oriental Silk," sales of the same color went up. Ivory, like "eye-ease" green, had developed a reputation for institutional blandness and boredom, but a romantic name gave it new appeal.

Patterns in fabric and wallpaper are also given names that evoke nostalgia and romantic images, for example, Camelot, Frolic, Flamingo, Hawaiian Paradise, Regency, and so on.

COLOR TRENDS

Part of your personal image is the belief that your views are shared by others (Boulding, 1966, p. 14), and enough people sharing a common image of interior color constitute a buying public. As the collective mood changes, trends are created and reflected in the marketplace. Trends are not static but change with more or less predictable regularity.

Although you may consider your color preferences uniquely individual, you very likely share the public mood, because you are a member of that public.

Whether you choose to follow the crowd or not, market availability will limit your color choices.

COLOR CYCLES

A "new" color is often introduced by the elite upper-end market, and if it catches the eye of a larger public, its use becomes more widespread. A dynamic bell curve goes into operation, during the course of which the color moves "from specialty retailers to department stores, then to higher volume sellers, mass merchants, and finally to low-end retailers" (Lamb in Linton, 1994, p. 63). Color products become popular, more available, and less expensive at the peak of the curve.

A trend in the fashion world can last 2 years, but in interior design it may take 7 to 12 years from the first appearance of a color until it is gone (Linton, 1994, p. 95). As the public mood shifts, new colors emerge and take center stage for a while; as one cycle comes to an end, another begins.

COLOR FORECASTING

Accurate forecasting of color trends is critical to manufacturers, who require approximately 2 years to make products in new colors. If the color forecasters are correct, you and millions of other consumers will like what is on the market and buy it. But if the color does not sell the merchandise, it is a flop, and someone loses money.

Color forecasters are alert to what is happening in the world today. They take into account occurrences that could affect public demand, such as:

- nuances of change in lifestyles, environments, design, and materials;
- events, such as the Bicentennial or the Olympics or a world's fair or the moon landing;
- people who influence public taste, such as Jacqueline Kennedy or Princess Diana;
- movements like the "green revolution" and environmental awareness;
- movements in the art world, such as op art or the retrospective exhibition of Monet's paintings;
- the influence of rock music and the drug culture as in the 1960s.

As you can see by looking around you, there are lingering evidences of past trends as well as colors in current vogue.

COLOR TRENDS AND THE PUBLIC MOOD

Color trends do not take place in a vacuum but occur in response to public currents of thought and feeling. Sharpe identifies color trends since the Victorian era:

- Murky shades of brown, red, lavender, and purple—the depressing colors of the Victorian period that reflected a repression of natural drives and a facade of piety, purity, and morality, a time of hypocrisy.

- A brief flash of color—magenta, bright orange, and violet—just before World War I, inspired by the Russian Ballet, but which never found wide popularity with the general public because of the lack of "a democracy of taste as we know it today" (Sharpe, 1974, p. 114).
- Khaki, tans, and grayish and olive greens during the dark days of World War I.
- Beige, gray, and medium blue along with brown and a combination of navy blue and white during the Roaring Twenties, thought to be expressive of the emotional letdown after the prolonged tension of the war.
- Rich dark wines, bottle greens, and chocolate browns relieved by white and light accents during the Great Depression of 1929–1939, thought to have fostered feelings of security in an insecure age.
- Neutral beiges, tans, and grays with scattered outbursts of brightness during World War II.
- The dominance of pastels, reflecting the strong influence of women during the 1950s.
- A riot of jarring colors in the 1960s when a new generation of designers and artists came into being—the rock music of the Beatles, the influence of LSD, the op art movement—all part of the revolution that liberated color from traditional restraints (Sharpe, 1974, pp. 113–116).

The influence of television programs should not be ignored—programs such as *Miami Vice* of the late 1970s and early 1980s, with its beach pastel pinks and aquas.

Charbonneau recalls the "avocado syndrome" as one of the most memorable trends, during the course of which "an avocado green haze crept into and onto everything," along with some orange and gold. This included large and small appliances, fabrics, carpets, rugs, resilient floors, and paints as well as "Mediterranean furniture" until people were "thoroughly sick of it" (Charbonneau in Linton, 1994, p. 101).

The next memorable surge was the infamous "earth tones craze" or the "lodge look," with emphasis on dark, heavy browns, orange, terra cotta, and other warm earth colors. Rustic furniture, the "twig" look, natural materials and textures, such as Haitian cotton fabrics, Berber carpeting, straw rattan, and wicker, became the rage. Shag carpeting, stucco-texture walls, and heavy rustic paneling and beams also characterized the era, along with the indoor use of exterior materials, such as brick, stone, and rough-sawn paneling (Charbonneau in Linton, 1994, pp. 101–102). Michelle Lamb states that the lodge look has been so successful because it symbolizes basic simplicity and home as refuge in an increasingly fast paced and complicated world. It is also a response to the interest in nature and the environment (Lamb in Linton, 1994, pp. 64–65).

However, the lodge look changed from cozy to depressing as people began to tire of dark, cavelike spaces. Pastels were introduced to liven things up—peaches, pinks, pale blues, greens, ivories, and creams looked fresh and new against the browns and earth colors (Charbonneau in Linton, 1994, p. 103).

This was followed by historic "traditional" color influences inspired by the 1976 Bicentennial. Muted shades of "Williamsburg" blues, greens, roses, and ivories complemented with reds and shades of putty and gold became popular. Growing out of this was the popular "country look." Gray replaced brown, and grayed tones of many colors became available. Rose and mauve gray with a "touch of teal" appeared not only in homes but in hotels, restaurants, offices, and medical facilities across the country (Charbonneau in Linton, 1994, p. 104).

The Color Marketing Group predicts "in" colors for 1997, complete with romantic names:

- Lime-light: soft veiled yellow-green
- Texas gold: metallic, muted gold
- Longhorn: deep reddish brown and grayish, red-cast brown
- Mediterraneo: bright energetic aquatic hue
- Clementine: midtone orange
- Silver spur: metallic techno-color, mineral gray
- Canyon cloud: metallic color, reminiscent of a morning mist
- Anemone: purple violet toward pink
- Vinaigrette: orange-cast purples
- Miss Ellie: powdery pink
- Red snapper: deep coral
- Sangria: bright burgundy (Freedman, 1996, p. 9)

Vestiges of many past trends are still with us, and if you are old enough or know what to look for, evidence of them can still be found. Color trends will continue to come and go, and people will continue to seek trendy colors for the places where they live and work. The cycle repeats itself.

The question any designer confronts is whether to take advantage of what is on the market or to seek that which is unique. Perhaps you may become known for your innovative uses of color and instigate a new trend.

BIBLIOGRAPHY

Albers, Josef. *Interaction of Color.* New Haven: Yale University Press, 1963.

Arnheim, Rudolf. *Art and Visual Perception.* Berkeley: University of California Press, 1954.

Barrett, Cyril. *An Introduction to Optical Art.* New York: Dutton, 1971.

Beck, Jacob. *Surface Color Perception.* Ithaca, NY: Cornell University Press, 1972.

Birren, Faber. *Color and Human Response,* rev. ed. New York: Van Nostrand Reinhold, 1978.

Birren, Faber. *Light, Color, and Environment.* New York: Van Nostrand Reinhold, 1982.

Bloomer, Carolyn M. *Principles of Visual Perception.* New York: Van Nostrand Reinhold, 1976.

Bornstein, Marc H., and Michael E. Lamb, Eds. *Developmental Psychology: An Advanced Textbook,* 2nd ed. Hillsdale, NJ: Lawrence Erlbaum, 1988.

Boulding, Kenneth E. *The Image: Knowledge in Life and Society.* Ann Arbor: Ann Arbor Paperbacks, University of Michigan Press, 1966.

Carter, John H. "The Effects of Aging on Selected Visual Functions: Color Vision, Glare Sensitivity, Field of Vision, and Accommodation" in R. Sekuler, D. Kline, and K. Dismukes, Eds., *Aging and Visual Function.* New York: Liss, 1982.

Charbonneau, Kenneth X. *"Color Forecasting—Mystery or Science?"* in Harold Linton, *Color Forecasting: A Survey of International Color Marketing.* New York: Van Nostrand Reinhold, 1994.

De Grandis, Luigina. *Theory and Use of Color.* Translated by John Gilbert. Englewood Cliffs, NJ: Prentice-Hall and New York: Abrams, 1984.

Faulkner, Ray, LuAnn Nissen, and Sarah Faulkner, *Inside Today's Home.* New York: Holt, Rinehart and Winston, 1986.

Fiske, Donald W., and Salvatore R. Maddi, Eds. *Functions of Varied Experience.* Homewood, IL: Dorsey Press, 1961.

Freedman, Jennifer, "Color Marketing Group: Colors that Will Sell in 1997," *Inter-society Color Council News,* No. 360, March/April, 1996.

Garau, Augusto. *Color Harmonies.* Chicago: University of Chicago Press, 1993.

Gardner, Carl, and Barry Hannaford. *Lighting Design.* New York: Wiley, 1993.

Gerritsen, Frans. *Theory and Practice of Color,* 2nd Ed. New York: Van Nostrand Reinhold, 1983.

Gibson, James J. *Perception of the Visual World.* Cambridge, MA: Riverside Press, 1950.

Gibson, James J. *The Senses Considered as Perceptual Systems.* Boston: Houghton Mifflin, 1966.

Gibson, James J. *The Ecological Approach to Visual Perception.* Boston: Houghton Mifflin, 1979.

Gordon, Gary, and James L. Nuckolls. *Interior Lighting for Designers,* 3rd ed. New York: Wiley, 1995

Gregory, R. L. *Eye and Brain: The Psychology of Seeing.* New York: McGraw-Hill, 1966.

Hubel, David H. *Eye, Brain, and Vision.* New York: Scientific American Library, 1995.

Illuminating Engineering Society of North America, Color Committee. *Color and Illumination* (DG-1). New York: IESNA, 1990.

Illuminating Engineering Society of North America, *Handbook,* 8th ed. New York: IESNA, 1993.

Itten, Johannes. *The Elements of Color.* New York: Van Nostrand Reinhold, 1970.

Kaufman, Donald, and Taffy Dahl. *Color: Natural Palettes for Painted Rooms.* New York: Potter, 1992.

Kuehni, Rolf G. *Color: Essence and Logic.* New York: Van Nostrand Reinhold, 1983.

Kwallek, N., and C. M. Lewis. "Effects of Environmental Colour on Males and Females: A Red or White or Green Office," *Applied Ergonomics,* 1980, Vol. 21.4, pp. 275–278.

Lamb, Michelle. "Trends in Color and Pattern" in Harold Linton. *Color Forecasting: A Survey of International Color Marketing.* New York: Van Nostrand Reinhold, 1994.

Lang, Jon. *Creating Architectural Theory.* New York: Van Nostrand Reinhold, 1987.

Langer, Susanne K. *Philosophy in a New Key.* New York: Mentor, 1951.

Linton, Harold, and Richard Rochon. *Color Model Environments.* New York: Van Nostrand Reinhold, 1985.

Linton, Harold, *Color Forecasting: A Survey of International Color Marketing.* New York: Van Nostrand Reinhold, 1994.

Linton, Harold, and Elsa Hämäläinen, Eds. *Aspects of Color.* Helsinki, Finland: The University of Art and Design, 1995.

Livingstone, Margaret S. "Art, Illusion and the Visual System," *Scientific American,* January 1988, Vol. 258, No. 1, pp. 78–85.

Mahnke, Frank H., and Rudolf H. Mahnke. *Color and Light in Man-Made Environments.* New York: Van Nostrand Reinhold, 1993.

Miller, Mary C. *Perceptual Foundations of Interior Design.* Ann Arbor: University Microfilm, 1971.

Mock, Elizabeth B. *If You Want to Build a House.* New York: Museum of Modern Art, 1946.

Moore, Fuller. *Concepts and Practice of Architectural Daylighting.* New York: Van Nostrand Reinhold, 1986.

The New Munsell Student Color Set. Philadelphia: Fairchild, 1994.

Nayar, Shree K., and Michael Oren. "Visual Appearance of Matte Surfaces," *Science,* February 24, 1995, Vol. 267, No. 5201.

"101 Questions and Answers About Paint and Painting." Devoe and Raynolds Co., 4000 Dupont Circle, Louisville, KY 40207.

Oberascher, Leonard. "Cyclic Recurrence of Collective Color References" in Harold Linton, *Color Forecasting: A Survey of International Color Marketing.* New York: Van Nostrand Reinhold, 1994.

Platt, John R. "Beauty, Pattern, and Change" in Donald W. Fiske and Salvatore R. Maddi, Eds. *Functions of Varied Experience.* Homewood, IL: Dorsey Press, 1961.

Rau, Richard P., and David G. Wright. *Beginning Design Courses at Schools of Architecture in Western Europe.* A Documentary Study. Cambridge, MA: Architecture Research Office, Harvard Graduate School of Design, 1975.

Sebastian, Pamela. *The Wall Street Journal,* February 8, 1996, Eastern Edition, p. 1.

Seitz, William C. *The Responsive Eye.* New York: Museum of Modern Art, 1965.

Sekuler, Robert, and Randolph Blake. *Perception,* 2nd ed. New York: Knopf, 1985.

Sekuler, Robert, and Randolph Blake. *Perception,* 3rd ed. New York: McGraw-Hill,

Sharpe, Deborah T. *The Psychology of Color and Design.* Totowa, NJ: Littlefield and Adams, 1974.

Swirnoff, Lois. *Dimensional Color.* Boston: Birkhäuser, 1988

Wong, Wucius. *Principles of Color Design.* New York: Van Nostrand Reinhold, 1987.

FACULTY WHO CONTRIBUTED EXAMPLES OF STUDENT WORK

Gephart, Robert, University of North Carolina at Greensboro.

Hasell, Dr. Joe, and Gerald Leimanstoll, Department of Interior Design, University of Cincinnati.

Hasell, Dr. Joe, School of Architecture, University of Florida, Gainsville, Florida.

Linton, Ralph, Lawrence Technological University.

Gretchen Rudy and Rochelle Martin, Lawrence Technological University.

CREDITS FOR COLOR ART

Color Art 1 Photograph by Mary Miller.

Color Art 2 From a student of Mary Jo Hasell and Jerry Leimenstoll, University of Cincinnati.

Color Art 3*A–D* From Harold Linton, *Color Model Environments,* Van Nostrand Reinhold, 1985, Plates 20-31. Reprinted with permission.

Color Art 4 © Tina Freeman, Photographer, Decatur Studio, Inc. Reprinted with permission.

Color Art 5 Reprinted with permission from Jason Weisenfeld, Director of Public Relations, Bloomingdale's, New York.

Color Art 6 Reprinted with permission from Dianca Quantrell, President, Quantrell Mullins & Associates, Inc., Atlanta, and Brian Robbins, Photographer.

Color Art 7 © Tina Freeman, Photographer, Decatur Studio, Inc. Reprinted with permission.

Color Art 8 Reprinted with permission from Quantrell Mullins & Associates, Inc., Atlanta, and Brian Robbins, Photographer.

Color Art 9 Photograph by Mary Miller.

Color Art 10 Reprinted with permission from Quantrell Mullins & Associates, Inc., Atlanta, and Jens Willebrand, Photographer.

Color Art 11 © National Trust Photo Library/Oliver Benn. Reprinted with permission.

Color Art 12 © Tina Freeman, Photographer, Decatur Studio, Inc. Reprinted with permission.

Color Art 13 Student works of Professors Gretchen Rudy and Rochelle Martin, College of Architecture and Design, Lawrence Technological University. From Harold Linton, *Aspects of Color.* Reprinted with permission.

Color Art 14 Courtesy of Weatherspoon Art Gallery, University of North Carolina, Greensboro.

Color Art 15 From a student of Professor Robert Gerhart, Art Department, University of North Carolina, Greensboro.

Color Art 16 Courtesy of Douglas Dreisphoon, Curator of Collections, Weatherspoon Art Gallery, University of North Carolina, Greensboro.

Color Art 17–21 Courtesy of Art Resource, New York. Reprinted with permission from Cooper–Hewitt National Design Museum, Smithsonian Institution.

Color Art 22*A–D* Student works of Professors Gretchen Rudy and Rochelle Martin, College of Architecture and Design, Lawrence Technological University. From Harold Linton, *Aspects of Color.* Reprinted with permission.

Color Art 23 Courtesy of Joe Crivy, Artist.

Color Art 24*A–B* Photographs by Mary Miller.

Color Art 25*A* Photograph by Mary Miller; source unknown.

Color Art 25*B* Courtesy of Robert Irwin, Artist.

Color Art 25*C* © 1984 Masahiro Chatani. Reprinted with permission from Greg MacCarthy, General Manager, AG Industry Co., Ltd., Redmond, Washington.

Color Art 25*D* Courtesy of Professor Clara Ridder, Department of Housing and Interior Design, University of North Carolina, Greensboro.

Color Art 26 Photograph by Mary Miller; source unknown.

Color Art 27 Courtesy of Robert Irwin, Artist.

Color Art 28 Reprinted with permission from Quantrell Mullins & Associates, Inc., Atlanta, and Timothy Hursley, Photographer.

Color Art 29*A–C* Experiments by Mary Miller.

Color Art 30 Courtesy of Professor In-Ouk Oh, Architect, Department of Interior Design, Kyungwon University.

Color Art 31 Courtesy of Professor Clara Ridder, Department of Housing and Interior Design, University of North Carolina, Greensboro.

Color Art 32*A* Reprinted with permission from Jack Fleming, General Manager, Stouffer's Hotel, Nashville.

Color Art 32*B* Courtesy of Professor In-Ouk Oh, Architect, Department of Interior Design, Kyungwon University.

Color Art 32*C* Courtesy of the state of Tennessee. Reprinted with permission from the Tennessee State Capitol Commission.

Color Art 33*A–E* Color plates by Mary Miller.

Color Art 34*A–D* Color plates by Mary Miller.

Color Art 35*A–C* Student of Professor Robert Gerhart, Art Department, University of North Carolina, Greensboro.

Color Art 36*A–D*, 37*A–B* Color plates by Mary Miller.

Color Art 38*A–B* Color slides by Mary Miller; fabrics woven by Mary Miller.

Color Art 39, 40 41*A–B* Courtesy of Art Resource, New York. Reprinted with permission from Cooper–Hewitt National Design Museum, Smithsonian Institution.

Color Art 41C Courtesy of Jack Lenore Larsen, Inc.

Color Art 42*A–G* Diagrams from Rudolf Arnheim, *Art and Visual Perception*, University of California Press, pp. 290–293. Reprinted with permission from University of California Press. Color plates by Mary Miller.

Color Art 43*A–C*, 44, 45, 46*A–X*, 47 Color plates by Mary Miller.

Color Art 48–50 Courtesy of Munsell Color, Macbeth, New Windsor, New York.

Color Art 51 Color plate by Mary Miller.

Color Art 52 © Tina Freeman, Photographer, Decatur Studio, Inc. Reprinted with permission.

Color Art 53 Reprinted with permission from Jennifer Yuracheck, Director of Community Relations, Wellspring Retirement Community, Greensboro, North Carolina.

Color Art 54 Reprinted with permission of Jo Hasell, University of Florida.

Color Art 55 Photograph by Mary Miller.

Color Art 56*A–E* Color plates by Mary Miller; photographed by Dan Smith, Learning Resources Center, University of North Carolina, Greensboro.

Color Art 57 Courtesy of Art Resource, New York. Reprinted with permission from Cooper–Hewitt National Design Museum, Smithsonian Institution.

Color Art 58 Photograph by Mary Miller; source unknown.

Color Art 59 Courtesy of Robert Irwin, Artist.

Color Art 60 Reprinted with permission of Cousins Properties, Inc.

Color Art 61 Owned by Mary Miller; origin unknown.

INDEX